In *The Biology of Sin*, Matthew S[...]ing interface between the spirit and the brain in ways that are sure to intrigue and stimulate those who are interested in how Christian faith can inform our understanding of a fallen corporeal nature. I enthusiastically recommend this book to all Christians who are curious about science.

Jeffrey M. Schwartz, M.D.
Research psychiatrist, UCLA School of Medicine and author of The Mind and the Brain: Neuroplasticity and the Power of Mental Force

Sin doesn't occur in a vacuum. We sin by choice, but our choices are often guided by inclinations that we often don't understand. Dr. Stanford has provided a valuable resource to the church by integrating a wide range of research on the biological conditions associated with various kinds of sins together with Scriptural teaching on these problems and how to address them. Avoiding the extremes of moralism and determinism, he takes seriously both human responsibility and biological vulnerabilities. Peppered with case studies, this book will be helpful to pastors, laypeople, and counselors seeking a better understanding of this complex area of human life.

Eric L. Johnson, Ph.D.
Lawrence and Charlotte Hoover Professor of Pastoral Care, Southern Baptist Theological Seminary and author of Foundations for Soul Care: A Christian Psychology Proposal

In years of trying to help people through the complex issues of their brokenness, I've longed for resources to help explain the power of innate sin in a person's life. Thank you, Matt, for integrating biology and brokenness so we can help set people free from the pains and struggles of their lives.

Jimmy Seibert
Pastor, Antioch Community Church (Waco, TX) and author of The Church Can Change the World: Living from the Inside Out

We both love how Matthew has taken the concept of sin and given a breath of fresh air to the topic. You must read this book because in its pages you will finally gain a biblical perspective on sin and what it takes to free yourself from the bonds that so easily entangle!

Gary and Michael Smalley
Smalley Relationship Center

The Biology of Sin

The Biology of Sin

of Sin

Grace, Hope, and Healing
for Those Who Feel Trapped

by

Matthew S. Stanford, Ph.D.

IVP Books

An imprint of InterVarsity Press
Downers Grove, Illinois

InterVarsity Press
P.O. Box 1400, Downers Grove, IL 60515-1426
World Wide Web: www.ivpress.com
Email: email@ivpress.com

InterVarsity Press® is the book-publishing division of InterVarsity Christian Fellowship/USA®, a movement of students and faculty active on campus at hundreds of universities, colleges and schools of nursing in the United States of America, and a member movement of the International Fellowship of Evangelical Students. For information about local and regional activities, write Public Relations Dept., InterVarsity Christian Fellowship/USA, 6400 Schroeder Rd., P.O. Box 7895, Madison, WI 53707-7895, or visit the IVCF website at www.intervarsity.org.

All Scripture quotations, unless otherwise indicated, are taken from the New American Standard Bible®, *copyright 1960, 1962, 1963, 1968, 1971, 1972, 1973, 1975, 1977, 1995 by The Lockman Foundation. Used by permission.*

Originally published by Biblica.

ISBN 978-0-8308-5613-8

Printed in the United States of America ∞

g green press *InterVarsity Press is committed to protecting the environment and to the responsible use of natural*
press *resources. As a member of Green Press Initiative we use recycled paper whenever possible. To learn*
INITIATIVE *more about the Green Press Initiative, visit www.greenpressinitiative.org.*

Library of Congress Cataloging-in-Publication Data is available through
the Library of Congress.

P	20	19	18	17	16	15	14	13	12	11	10	9	8	7	6
Y	30	29	28	27	26	25	24	23	22	21	20	19			

CONTENTS

Chapter 1

Crouching at the Door

Sin is crouching at the door;
and its desire is for you, but you must master it.
—Genesis 4:7

I have seen the dark side of humanity. As a neuroscientist studying impulsive and aggressive behavior, I have sat across an interview table from countless murderers, rapists, and drug addicts. What has struck me the most over the years, however, is how ordinary these individuals are. People who have done very evil things are more like you and me than we may want to admit. Most have dreamed of better lives for themselves and desperately want to change but don't know how. Back when I was a young graduate student, I had imagined that such people would be

monsters—grotesque and frightening. What I have found over the years is
that they are more pitiful and lost than they are terrifying.

Privately, we are quick to compare our bad behavior to those around
us. If we can just find someone worse than us, then somehow that makes
our bad behavior not so bad. *I've never killed anyone, so that makes me better
than the murderer. I'm not dependent on alcohol or drugs, so that makes me
better than the addict.*

But how bad is *too* bad, and by what standard should we be judged?
God has called his people to "be holy," as he is holy (Leviticus 19:2). He
requires moral perfection, and we fall miserably short (Romans 3:23).
Without Christ, we are all the same. Our human labels are meaningless—
whether they be "murderer," "rapist," "drug addict," or "neuroscientist." We
are all spiritually dead and separated from God.

Sin is a ruthless beast: crouching at the door, waiting to consume us
all (Genesis 4:7). When we encounter those whom it has overcome, we
should feel sorrow rather than self-righteous pride. Sitting across the table
from impulsive and aggressive patients is more like looking into a mirror
than gazing at a monster. I see my own imperfections, the stain of sin, and
I am grateful for God's abundant grace (Romans 5:17; Ephesians 1:7–8).
A pastor friend of mine often says he has never met a person that Christ
didn't die for. Each time I sit down at the interview table, I am reminded
that I haven't either.

DEFINING THE PROBLEM

What is sin? If you ask ten people that question, you are likely to get ten
different answers. In fact, some might even respond that there is no such
thing. That's because we often view sin as a matter of breaking the rules. But
what set of rules should we use as our standard: the Ten Commandments,
the Code of Hammurabi, the federal laws of the United States? What if
your set of rules differs from mine? Can behavior that you consider sinful
be acceptable behavior for me?

The Bible uses a number of Hebrew and Greek words that we translate as "sin," but two are most common: *chata* and *hamartia*. In the Old Testament, the Hebrew word *chata* (e.g., Exodus 20:20) is used most often to describe sin. *Chata* means "miss," as in to miss a target. The same word is used in Judges 20:16 to describe a group of left-handed warriors from the tribe of Benjamin who could "sling a stone at a hair and not *miss*" (emphasis added). In the New Testament, the most common Greek word used to describe sin is *hamartia*, which means "to miss the mark." Paul used this word when he wrote, in Romans 3:23, that "all have sinned and fall short of the glory of God." This verse could also be translated, "All have *missed the mark* and fall short of the glory of God." *Sin, then, is best defined as missing, or falling short, of the glory of God.*

To better understand what sin is, we must have a greater appreciation for the glory of God.

THE GLORY OF GOD

The glory of God is mentioned throughout the biblical text, both the Old Testament and the New Testament (e.g., Exodus 24:17; Revelation 21:23). At its appearance, individuals—whether prophets (Ezekiel 1:28), priests (1 Kings 8:11), kings (2 Chronicles 7:1–3), or lowly shepherds (Luke 2:9)—fell to the ground in fear and awe. God's glory is continually referred to by choirs of angels before the throne of heaven (Isaiah 6:3; Revelation 5:11–12), and it is purposely reflected in the created universe so that human beings might know God (Psalm 19:1; Romans 1:18–25).

To look fully upon God's glory is to see the very face of God, to see him as he truly is. In the dark time after the Israelites' sin of making and worshiping the golden calf, followed then by the destruction of the first set of tablets inscribed with the Ten Commandments, Moses, questioning his ability to lead the people, cried out to God, "Show me Your glory!" (Exodus 33:18). God agreed, yet he cautioned Moses that no one could look upon his full glory and live. However, he hid Moses in a cleft in the rock and covered him with his protective hand. Passing by, he allowed Moses to see the afterglow of his glory.

As God passed by the hidden and protected Moses, he proclaimed his glory aloud, "The LORD, the LORD God, compassionate and gracious, slow to anger, and abounding in lovingkindness and truth; who keeps lovingkindness for thousands, who forgives iniquity, transgression and sin; yet He will by no means leave the guilty unpunished, visiting the iniquity of fathers on the children and on the grandchildren to the third and fourth generations" (Exodus 34:6–7).

The glory of God is the sum total of who he is: his divine nature, attributes, characteristics, powers, and abilities all together. And as I mentioned above, it is also the standard by which sin is defined (Romans 3:23). The glory of God is the standard for our every thought and action. Whatever we do, it is to be done to the glory of God (1 Corinthians 10:31). Evaluated in this way, sin seems to be more a state of being than a set of wrong thoughts and behaviors that should be avoided.

To be fully aware of sin's destructive power, we need to go back to the beginning—to where it all started.

THE ORIGIN OF SIN

Before Adam and Eve were created, before there was an Eden or a forbidden tree, sin began to burn in the heart of a holy angel. The name Satan comes from a Hebrew word (*satan*) that means "adversary," "accuser," or "opponent." In Isaiah's prophecy against the king of Babylon, the prophet seems to go beyond the scope of a human king and describe the fall of Satan. "How you have fallen from heaven, O star of the morning, son of the dawn! You have been cut down to the earth, you who have weakened the nations!" (Isaiah 14:12). The Hebrew for "star of the morning" was translated "Lucifer" in an early Latin translation of the Bible.

A similar situation is found in Ezekiel 28. Though the immediate context of this prophecy was in regard to the king of Tyre, the Lord, through

Ezekiel, apparently goes beyond addressing a human king to describe Satan: "You had the seal of perfection, full of wisdom and perfect in beauty. You were in Eden, the garden of God; every precious stone was your covering. . . . You were the anointed cherub who covers, and I placed you there. You were on the holy mountain of God; you walked in the midst of the stones of fire. You were blameless in your ways from the day you were created until unrighteousness was found in you. . . . Your heart was lifted up because of your beauty; you corrupted your wisdom by reason of your splendor" (Ezekiel 28:12–17).

Prideful because of his beauty and position, Satan (Lucifer) questioned God's sovereignty. Desiring equality with the Creator, he thought to himself, "I will ascend to heaven; I will raise my throne above the stars of God, and I will sit on the mount of assembly in the recesses of the north. I will ascend above the heights of the clouds; I will make myself like the Most High" (Isaiah 14:13–14). Gathering to his side other angels willing to question the sovereignty of the Almighty, he rebelled. Second Peter 2:4 mentions the angels (plural) who sinned, leading to the conclusion that there were many other angels who assisted Satan in his rebellion and were therefore banished from heaven.

The Greek term *diabolos* (devil), sometimes used to refer to Satan in the New Testament, means "slanderer," "traitor," or "false accuser." The New Testament writers employed a number of different terms to refer to Satan: "the tempter," "the evil one," "Beelzebul," "the ruler of the demons," "the enemy," and "the ruler of this world."

The story of Satan's fall is a tragic tale of pride's destructive power. But can the blame for sin entering the world be placed solely on Satan? In the section on sin in his small catechism, Martin Luther asks the question, "By whom was sin brought into the world?" His answer is short and to the point: "Sin was brought into the world by the *devil*, who was once a holy angel but fell away from God, and by *man*, who of his own free will yielded to the temptation of the devil (1 John 3:8; Romans 5:12)" (emphasis added).[1] While Satan indeed fell first and certainly played a major role in the fall of humanity, in a very real sense we are coconspirators with him. Both parties have paid a heavy price for their rebellion.

THE FALL OF MAN

Man is unlike any other living creature that God created. While all living creatures, including man, were formed from the ground of the earth (Genesis 2:7, 19), only man was created in the image of God (Genesis 1:26).[2] Even more amazing is that God breathed into the newly formed man and he became a living being (Genesis 2:7). Like God, our true essence is spirit, meaning that we can be in an intimate relationship with our Creator.

God placed the man and woman in a literal paradise on earth, Eden (Genesis 2:8), and provided for their every need. Like he had done with the angels, God gave the man and woman free will and allowed them to make decisions for themselves. Created spiritually innocent and sinless, Adam and Eve knew an intimacy with God that we can only imagine (Genesis 3:8). They were in perfect harmony with their Creator and with each other (Genesis 2:25). He had given them life and provided for their every need. He was their daily companion—their friend—and he dearly loved them. In Eden, all things were possible, and only a single behavior was forbidden: they were told never to eat the fruit from "the tree of the knowledge of good and evil." If they did, God said that they would die (Genesis 2:17).

How long this perfect union of God and humankind lasted, we have no idea. Ultimately it doesn't really matter, because a day came when Satan entered the garden. Cast down from heaven, unable to have the throne of the Most High, in his hatred and rage toward God he chose to hurt the Creator by attacking his most beloved creation—man. Approaching the woman, Satan questioned the motives of God's command not to eat from the forbidden tree. In fact, in an ironic twist Satan deceived Eve into committing the same sin that had caused him to be cast out: desiring equality with God (Genesis 3:5). So she ate, and then Adam ate, and then everything changed.

Instead of being in a harmonious, loving relationship with their Creator, they now feared him and hid themselves (Genesis 3:8). Spiritually, they were now separated from him. God removed his protective hand and cast them out of Eden, leaving them at the mercy of the elements. Food and water were hard to come by; childbirth was painful; it was difficult to maintain harmony in their marital and family relationships; their bodies began to age; they would get sick; and ultimately they would die. Never was this more evident and painful than when one of their children (Cain) killed his brother (Abel) out of anger and jealousy (Genesis 4:3–8). Like Satan, questioning the sovereignty of God by desiring equality with the Creator had cost Adam and Eve everything, and sin was now in the world.

TYPES OF SIN

There are basically two types of sin: *original sin* and *actual sin*. Original sin is also called *inherited sin*, because it was passed down to us by our father Adam. But how can I be held responsible for something this Adam guy did long before I was born? Well, like it or not, it's true. Furthermore, if we are going to reconcile the biological and spiritual aspects of sinful behaviors, such as drunkenness and homosexuality, it is essential that we have a correct understanding of the doctrine of original sin.

Adam, as the first man, has a twofold relationship to all his descendants (including you and me). First, he was the natural head of the human race, the biological father of all human beings. To this physical relationship God added a covenant relationship, by virtue of which Adam was also the representative of all his descendants (you and me, again). A covenant is a binding agreement between two parties, in this instance God and humankind. When Adam sinned in his representative capacity, the guilt of his sin was passed on to all those whom he represented. As a result, we are all born in a sinful state. "Just as through one man sin entered into the world, and death through sin, and so death spread to all men, because all sinned" (Romans 5:12). Through this covenant relationship, we all share in what could be called "original guilt" and are accountable before God for the sin of Adam. At birth we are spiritually dead, separated from God with no hope of spiritual life.

But remember that the results of sin were also biological for Adam and Eve. They began to change physically; the consequences were aging, sickness, and death. We have also inherited from Adam, our biological father, a physical aspect of sin, what I like to call "sinful DNA." As a result of our sinful biology at birth, our physical and mental inclinations are only for self, and as we grow they continue to be self-focused. In relation to God, there is simply no good in us, neither spiritually nor physically. Our fundamental preference is toward sin (Psalm 51:5; Romans 7:18, 8:7). It is out of a mind and body corrupted by original sin that actual sins come forth.

An actual sin is a thought or behavior that violates a commandment of God (1 John 3:4). Actual sins are the "Thou shalt nots"—like lying, cheating, and stealing—that people of faith try to avoid. In fact, this is how we most often think and talk about sin, as bad behaviors to avoid. Much like the rich young ruler who asked Jesus what he should do to inherit eternal life (Mark 10:17–20), we gauge our personal holiness, or how acceptable we are to God, by the number of actual sins we do or do not commit. I can tell you from personal experience; that approach to living the Christian life always ends in frustration and failure.

Let's not forget, sin is falling short of God's glory. We are born disqualified from life with God because of original sin. But let's say for a moment that original sin did not exist. Imagine that you were born like Adam and Eve, innocent and sinless. Would you be able to live your life devoid of actual sins—a life with no thoughts, words, or actions that fall short of God's glory? Remember, God requires moral perfection of his people (Leviticus 19:2), and even a single sin would disqualify you from life with him (James 2:10).

The Pharisees of Jesus' day were up for the challenge. They saw themselves as the most righteous of the Israelites. They lived their lives by a strict code of dos and don'ts that they thought brought them favor with God. In the Sermon on the Mount, Jesus said that a righteousness greater than that of the Pharisees was required for a person to enter into the kingdom of heaven (Matthew 5:20). And then he described what being holy like God really looks like. "You have heard that the ancients were told, 'You shall not commit murder' and 'Whoever commits murder shall be liable to the court.' But I say to you that everyone who is angry with his brother shall be guilty before the court; and whoever says to his brother, 'You good-for-nothing,' shall be guilty before the supreme court; and whoever says, 'You fool,' shall be guilty enough to go into the fiery hell" (Matthew 5:21–22).

Jesus likely chose this commandment because the Pharisees present during his teaching had never murdered anyone. By expanding on this commandment, Jesus shows us two important things about sin. First, sin begins in the mind long before the actual sinful act is committed (James 1:14–15). Second, there is no difference in the "seriousness" of sins in God's eyes; to him, sin is sin. Any sin, regardless of how trivial we may considerate it, disqualifies us from life with God. The Scriptures even teach us that it is possible to sin unintentionally—to not know that we have sinned—but still to be held accountable before God (Leviticus 4:2–3; Numbers 15:28).

Now the average life span for a person born in the United States today is seventy-seven years.[3] Are you up to the challenge: Could you live a sinless life? Adam and Eve were unsuccessful. The Pharisees tried and failed. And I'm also confident that neither you nor I would be successful.

RECONCILIATION

Is there any hope for us? Even if we weren't born with the guilt of original sin upon us, how could we ever meet the standard of sinless perfection necessary for life with God? Thankfully, someone else has met the standard for us; and he offers us the opportunity, through faith, to be forgiven and made new (Ephesians 2:8–9).

In the fullness of time, the Father sent the long-prophesied Savior, Jesus, to set us free from sin (Genesis 3:15; Isaiah 7:14). Conceived by the Holy Spirit and born of a virgin (Matthew 1:18), he did not share in the guilt of original sin. After living a sinless life, Jesus offered himself as a perfect sacrifice and took upon himself the punishment for sin that was meant for us (Romans 6:23; Ephesians 5:2). Satisfying God's wrath against sin, he was raised from the dead and exalted to the right hand of God the Father (Acts 2:32–33). Through faith in Jesus Christ, we are offered forgiveness of our sins (past, present, and future), a new living spirit, and the opportunity to be in an intimate spiritual union with our Creator.

SIN AND SCIENCE

It seems that you can't pick up a magazine or turn on the television these days without seeing a story on the conflict between science and religious belief. The disagreement tends to focus around three main issues: the sanctity of life, the origin of life, and sinful behavior. The *sanctity of life* includes topics such as abortion, euthanasia (i.e., physician-assisted suicide), the use of embryonic stem cells, and cloning. The second point of contention, the *origin of life*, is seen in the ongoing dispute between the proponents of naturalistic evolution and those who believe the universe shows signs of intelligent design. The third point of conflict has to do with biblically defined *sinful behavior* for which science has shown some biological predisposition or basis. Some of the most emotionally debated behaviors include homosexuality, addiction, and criminality. The purpose of this book is to speak to this third point of debate and, I hope, bring some resolution to the conflict.

The behaviors that will be discussed have been chosen for two reasons: first, because the Scriptures, which I consider the inspired and authoritative Word of God, clearly define them as sinful; and second, because the scientific community has traditionally addressed these behaviors as disorders.[4] There is no thought of judgment or condemnation toward those who might be struggling with these sins, but simply a desire that all will come away with a better understanding that our only hope is God's grace and absolute dependence on the risen Christ.

As a Christian and a neuroscientist, I stand at the boundary point of what appears, at least on the surface, to be two very different worlds—or perhaps it is more precise to say two very different worldviews. From my unique vantage point, I unfortunately have seen scientific knowledge distorted to justify sinful behavior; and perhaps more disturbingly, I have seen Christians misuse the Scriptures to demonize and alienate the very ones to whom they should be reaching out. The underlying cause of this problem in the church is a lack of knowledge, both of basic brain function and of scriptural teaching. It is my hope that this book will give you a better understanding of both.

WHY MEN?

If we look at the sins to be discussed in the following chapters, we find that men are more frequently involved than women in these behaviors. So the question must be asked, Do men and women sin differently? I believe they do, and I suggest that this is just one more piece of evidence that sin has biological roots.

Physiologically, men and women are very different. As I will describe throughout this book, it is often extremes (both highs and lows) in the same hormonal and biochemical systems that differ between the sexes, predisposing us to sinful behavior (e.g., lust). God made the sexes different but complementary (Genesis 2:18–25). He instilled certain drives and de-sires in the man, so that he might fulfill his divinely determined masculine role. A different set of female-specific drives and desires was created in the woman so that she might accomplish her God-ordained purposes.

Psychological science has long recognized these differences. For ex-ample, research has consistently found that women tend to have better ver-bal abilities than men and are relationally oriented, while men have better spatial or analytical skills and are task oriented. These cognitive differences have been linked to neurochemical, hormonal, and structural differences in the brains of men and women. The complementary nature of these dif-ferences changed when sin entered the world. Humankind became selfish and independent, with each individual relying only on himself or herself to fulfill their natural desires and physical appetites.

The gender differences observed in sinful behavior are foreshadowed in the curse that God pronounced upon Adam and Eve in the garden (Genesis 3:16–19). The man is told that he will have great difficulty in providing for himself and his family. So the sins most often committed by men tend to be outwardly manifested and focused on obtaining immediate pleasure or gratification (e.g., aggression). The curse upon the woman was that she would no longer be in an equivalent relationship with the man and that he would rule over her. Therefore the sins of women tend to be more inwardly focused and concern relational status, privilege, or position (e.g., envy). The neurobiological correlates of these inwardly focused types of sinful behavior are just now beginning to be investigated.[5]

A recent Catholic survey supports this idea that men and women sin differently. The study was based on the confessions heard by ninety-five-year-old Jesuit priest Roberto Busa after a lifetime in the priesthood and was focused on the traditional seven deadly sins: pride, envy, gluttony, lust, anger, greed, and sloth. The most common sins reported by men were lust and gluttony (sins related to immediate pleasure and gratification), while women were more likely to struggle with pride and envy (sins related to relational status and privilege).[6]

God has created us as embodied spirits, having physical and spiritual aspects to our being. Deeply stained and scarred by original sin, both spiritually and physically, we are at birth separated from God and incomplete. Because God created men and women physically different, it is understandable that the effect of original sin on our bodies and minds varies between the sexes. This is not to say that men and women differ in their degree of sinfulness, but simply that they tend to sin in different ways. Men and women are equally sinful, and sin is equally destructive in both. Through faith in Christ, we are transformed spiritually, but like all the physical creation, our bodies still long to be redeemed and made new (Romans 8:20–23). While salvation occurs in an instant, sanctification—the process by which our bodies and minds are formed into Christ's likeness—is a lifelong process that will only be fully realized at Christ's second coming.

Chapter 2

Alive for the First Time

The mind set on the flesh is death,
but the mind set on the Spirit is life and peace.
—Romans 8:6

B rain Day has become an annual tradition at my children's
school. On that day I bring a variety of brain specimens for
all the students to see and touch. There are certain advantages
(or disadvantages, depending on your perspective) to having a father who
is a neuroscientist. I like to bring the brains of several different animal species, such as rats, rabbits, and sheep, for the children to see and compare.
Of course, the most anticipated specimen is always the human brain.
Students, teachers, and administrators all crowd into the small classroom
just to get a peek at what is the most amazing piece of bioengineering that

will ever exist. The students' questions range from the curious ("Did you kill someone to get that brain?") to the complex ("How do we dream?"). It is a day that makes a lasting impression on the kids. "I touched a human brain today—cool!"

Much like those young children, I have always been fascinated by the human brain. From my undergraduate days, learning the anatomy of the sheep brain in class, to now teaching neuroscience doctoral students human neuroanatomy, I continue to marvel at the complexity of this three-pound miracle of creation.

The human brain contains approximately 100 billion neurons. It is 75 percent water and uses electricity and chemicals to form and store thoughts, feelings, and memories. The brain uses 20 percent of the body's energy but makes up only 2 percent of the body's weight. When awake, the human brain can generate up to 25 watts of power, enough to illuminate a light bulb. Information travels through its neural pathways at speeds of up to 120 meters per second (268 miles per hour)! Humans have the most complex brain of any living creature God has created on earth.

While the complexity of our brain may separate us from the other living creatures, that difference is only a matter of degree. Animals also have brains, and they work very much like our own. God created all living creatures, including human beings, from the ground of the earth (Genesis 2:7, 19), so it is not surprising that humans and animals are physically quite similar. What makes us fundamentally different from animals, however, is the fact that our true essence—that is, who we really are—is not a physical body but an immaterial spirit (2 Corinthians 5:1–4).

HOW WE WERE CREATED

You and I are not an accident or a chance biological occurrence (Psalm 139:13–16). We were created for the purpose of glorifying God (Isaiah 43:7), who has laid out a divine plan for each of our lives (Proverbs 16:9; Jeremiah 10:23, 29:11). The Scriptures teach us that we are a complex being, having both a physical (material) nature and a nonphysical (immaterial) nature (1 Thessalonians 5:23). We are the union of a physical body with an immaterial mind and spirit. To be able to understand fully the role that biology plays in sinful behavior, it is necessary that we have an understanding of the three-part unity of man: body, mind, and spirit.

Body

We exist in a physical body so that we can interact with the material world around us. Our bodies have been specifically designed to take in information from the environment and relay it to our brains. We see, hear, taste, smell, and touch the world around us. The processing of sensory information by our brains produces thoughts, feelings, and emotions, which then result in some outward behavioral display.

Paul refers to the body as an "earthly tent" (2 Corinthians 5:1–4) and makes it clear that we are more than physical (2 Corinthians 5:8). Indeed, we are more than simply a brain riding around in a body. There is an immaterial, nonphysical aspect to our being—what some would call our soul or mind.

Mind

Are our thoughts, feelings, and emotions merely the product of neurochemical changes and electrical discharges in our brain? Or is our mind something more—something immaterial, more than the sum of our parts? The truth is probably somewhere in the middle. While the functioning of our brain is integral to the existence of our mind, that alone is not sufficient to explain it. Similarly, to imagine our mind as completely separate and unrelated to the physical doesn't seem correct either. Mind and body are intimately connected, and each affects the other.

It is in our mind that we interact with God through prayer (1 Corinthians 14:15), receive divine revelation (Luke 24:45), and are transformed by the indwelling Holy Spirit (Romans 12:2). It is also in our mind that we choose to sin (Romans 8:6–7; 2 Corinthians 10:5). A physical body formed by the hands of the Maker in union with an immaterial mind that controls and plans our behavior is a truly miraculous—and perhaps difficult—idea to grasp. And the Scriptures teach us that we also have a third and even more amazing level of being: a spirit.

Spirit

God created us as three-part beings. In our inmost being we are spirit, the very breath of God placed into a shell of dust (Genesis 2:7; Ecclesiastes 12:6–7). As spirit beings, it is possible for us to be in an intimate spiritual union (Proverbs 20:27; Romans 8:15–16) with our Creator, who is also spirit (John 4:24). No other living creature, not even the angels, has been given such an opportunity.

Let's look at a simple visual representation to better understand the interaction between body, mind, and spirit. Figure 1 shows the body, mind, and spirit in relation to one another, each separate but interacting with the one above and/or below. The brain, via the body's sensory systems, is in

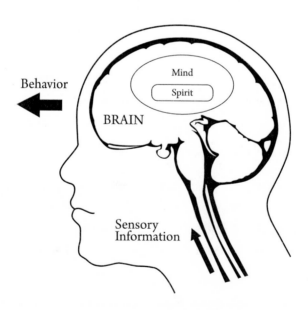

Figure 1. The Three-Part Unity of Man

contact with the earthly environment (outside) and the mind within. The middle ellipse is the mind, which is connected to the body through the functions of the brain and nervous system but also in contact with our immaterial spirit (the innermost rectangle). The body senses and reacts to the external environment, and the mind uses that information to perceive, understand, and interpret our surroundings. The mind also forms our thoughts and plans out our actions. The spirit, when connected to God, works to transform the mind into the very image of Christ, which results in an ever-increasing display of godly behaviors through the body (2 Corinthians 3:18).

We are the masterpiece of creation (Ephesians 2:10): the physical interacting with the immaterial, the Creator of the universe in communion with his beloved creation. That is how we were created, and that is how it was supposed to be. But we sinned, and the consequences of our disobedience are felt every day—both spiritually and physically.

THE EFFECTS OF THE FALL

God had been very clear: "In the day that you eat from it [the tree of the knowledge of good and evil] you will surely die" (Genesis 2:17; see also Genesis 3:3). The expression in the Hebrew text is to be understood as "*when* you eat from it" or "*as soon as* you eat from it." There is the sense of an immediate result from eating the fruit, and that result was death. But is that what happened? Did Adam and Eve die immediately?

When we look at Genesis, we see that something did happen immediately to Adam and Eve when they ate the forbidden fruit. "She took from its fruit and ate; and she gave also to her husband with her, and he ate. Then the eyes of both of them were opened, and they knew that they were naked; and they sewed fig leaves together and made themselves loin coverings" (Genesis 3:6–7). Christians traditionally have separated the ideas of spiritual death and physical death to explain the immediate and long-term consequences of Adam and Eve's sin. To better understand what God meant by death, we must first understand what it is to be alive.

Life and death are clearly opposites, like black and white or up and down. You are either one or the other; they are mutually exclusive categories, and there is no middle ground. Since God said that Adam and Eve died when they ate the forbidden fruit, the logical thought is that they must have been alive before they ate it. So what was "life" like for Adam and Eve? We know from Genesis that God provided for all their needs, from physical needs such as food and water (Genesis 2:16) to emotional needs like love and acceptance (Genesis 2:18). They were fully dependent on God for all things, and that dependence resulted in a level of spiritual intimacy that is summed up in the idea that God "walked" with them in the garden (Genesis 3:8). Imagine what it would be like to "walk" with God every day in a perfect, sinless paradise—to hear his voice, to feel his presence, to have no wants but to be fully satisfied, to be in such an intimate spiritual union with God that you share his thoughts and experience his perfect, unconditional love moment by moment. No fear. No pain. Now that is life!

Immediately upon Adam and Eve eating the fruit, the spiritual union that they had with God was severed. They were now on their own. We see that when the text tells us that "the eyes of both of them were opened, and they knew that they were naked" (Genesis 3:7). They were now disconnected from the true source of all life. They were empty and incomplete. Fearful and shamed by their very being, they sought to cover themselves and hide from the presence of God (Genesis 3:7–8). Existence from this point forward would be a constant struggle to try to meet unfulfilled needs and uncontrollable wants. In a very real sense, Adam and Eve had died. To be physically alive but spiritually dead, separated from the life-giver, is death. The only life that truly matters is life with God.

LIFE WITHOUT GOD

In Adam we are all dead, separated from God. We may be physically alive at birth, but we are spiritually dead. We are born with an imperfect body, scarred as the result of generations of sin. Left to fend for ourselves in a hostile and fallen world, we are at the mercy of the environment and biological processes that wreak havoc on our bodies and minds. Look at Figure 2 to get a better idea of how and why we think and act the way we do from birth.

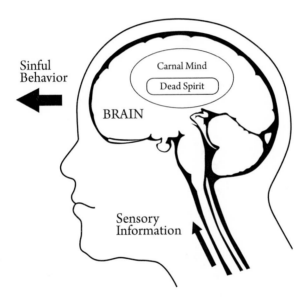

Figure 2. The Effects of the Fall on Man

As we grow and mature, our body and mind learn to interact with and react to our fallen environment, all the while spiritually separated from

God by our sin. The body, physically affected by sin, gathers sensory information from the worldly environment. Our carnal mind, knowing only sin because of our separation from God (dead spirit), chooses to satisfy itself by what we in psychology would call the pleasure principle, or the "if it feels good do it" lifestyle. In doing so, our mind associates normal physiological reactions and sensations with lustful desires and selfish wants (James 1:14–15). Emotionally, we are empty and unsatisfied, in a constant search for a source that might fill the void within us.

It is in our mind that we choose to sin (Romans 8:6–7), and it is with our body that we act out our sinful thoughts (Ephesians 2:3). In addition to the sinful drives and desires that control us, a result of sin was physical death and decay. In fact, the Scriptures tell us that the whole of the physical creation was affected by our sin and longs for the day of redemption (Romans 8:19–21). Our bodies are damaged because of sin. We age. We get sick. We suffer physically and die because the physical creation has been affected by the fall.

ABUNDANT LIFE

We are spiritually dead at birth, but we still have an eternally existing spirit—the spirit we received from Adam, a spirit eternally separated from God. Like the dry bones of Ezekiel 37, we need to be resurrected, brought back to life. That is exactly why Jesus came to earth. "I came that they may have life, and have it abundantly" (John 10:10). Jesus is the source and giver of life. When we come to faith in him, that dead, separated spirit is nailed to the cross with Christ, never to return (Galatians 2:20). In its place, the Spirit of Christ takes up residence in us (Galatians 4:6; Colossians 3:1–3). We are alive for the first time—in spiritual union with God! The believer is complete in Christ; we have everything we need for life and godliness in him (2 Peter 1:3). But what happens to our body and mind after we are transformed in our spirit?

Let's look at Figure 3 to help understand our new life in Christ. In the innermost area we now see a living spirit in union with Christ. The

Scriptures teach us that we are to submit ourselves to Christ and allow him to renew our minds (Romans 12:2). As our minds are renewed and our thoughts are taken captive to Christ (2 Corinthians 10:5), he begins to take control of our biological drives and impulses (Colossians 3:5–10), and our behavior changes.

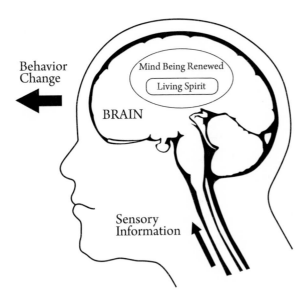

Figure 3. The Results of Spiritual Rebirth

THE FLESH

Unfortunately, we come to this new spiritual union with a significant amount of sinful baggage. Born damaged by sin, we lived some period of time before coming to Christ. As a result of living separated from God, we have developed immoral desires, distorted drives, corrupt thought patterns, and sinful habits.[1] The Scriptures refer to these old ways of trying to meet our needs as the "flesh" or "the law of sin" (Romans 7:18, 25).

In Galatians 5:19–21 we find a partial list of these sinful thoughts and behaviors: "Now the deeds of the flesh are evident, which are: immorality, impurity, sensuality, idolatry, sorcery, enmities, strife, jealousy, outbursts of anger, disputes, dissensions, factions, envying, drunkenness, carousing, and things like these." The "deeds of the flesh" listed here fall into four basic categories: sexual sins (immorality, impurity, sensuality), religious sins (idolatry, sorcery), social evils (enmities, strife, jealousy, outbursts of anger, disputes, dissensions, factions, envying), and sins associated with alcohol (drunkenness, carousing).[2] It is clear that this is not meant to be an exhaustive list of fleshly behavior, given Paul's concluding phrase: "and things like these."

While Paul originally wrote to a first-century audience, these sins are as much a problem today, in the twenty-first century, as they were in the early church. (Several of these sins will be discussed in later chapters.) Unfortunately, these sinful thoughts and behaviors don't simply disappear because we have been given a new life in Christ. But the good news is that change is now possible, whereas before our spiritual transformation it was not.

Each moment of the day, our mind now has a choice of how to respond. Either we will submit to the guidance of the indwelling Spirit, or we will choose our old, independent patterns of behavior (Romans 8:6). We will trust and submit to Christ to meet our needs, or we will choose to go it alone in our own strength. Notice how Paul, in Romans 7:18–23, describes this internal conflict in his own life:

> For I know that nothing good dwells in me, that is, in my flesh; for the willing is present in me, but the doing of the good is not. For the good that I want, I do not do, but I practice the very evil that I do not want. But if I am doing the very thing I do not want, I am no longer the one doing it, but sin which dwells in me. I find then the principle that evil is present in me, the

one who wants to do good. For I joyfully concur with the law of God in the inner man, but I see a different law in the members of my body, waging war against the law of my mind and making me a prisoner of the law of sin which is in my members.

Each day, in every situation, we must die to our old self (Luke 9:23; Ephesians 4:22–24) by choosing to live according to the Spirit. It is only through submission to Christ that our minds can be renewed and our lives forever transformed (Romans 12:1–2; Ephesians 4:23). Choosing to follow our flesh is contrary to our new nature; it simply isn't who we are anymore. Our old patterns may feel comfortable, even temporarily pleasurable, but we must not live contrary to who we are in Christ.

A NEW CREATION

In Christ we have been fundamentally changed! What we were before Christ no longer exists (2 Corinthians 5:17; Galatians 2:20). In Christ we were chosen before the foundation of the world; predestined for adoption as a child of the living God; purchased out of slavery to sin and death; forgiven of all our sins—past, present, and future; given spiritual wisdom and revelation; and marked as such until the day that we stand before God holy and blameless (Ephesians 1:3–14). That is who we are in Christ, and that is how we should now live.

If you have received Christ by faith, you are a holy, righteous child of God—even if you are struggling with habitual sin or fleshly behavior. Spiritually, you are complete in him and seated with him at the right hand of God Almighty (Ephesians 1:20, 2:6). It's your choice. How will you live? Will you live out of who you are—a child of the King—or will you choose to live contrary to your new nature and be a slave to sin and death?

FINAL THOUGHTS

I hope this chapter has shown you that sin is pervasive and affects us at every level of our being: body, mind, and spirit. Both believers and nonbelievers carry around the physical and mental effects of sinful pro-gramming. Fortunately, believers have been transformed inwardly and are righteous before God. But that doesn't instantaneously remove the bad "flesh" that we still carry. Sanctification is a long-term process by which our minds are continually being renewed through daily submission to Christ. Abnormal biological predispositions, corrupt thought patterns, and sinful desires do not simply go away by themselves once we come to faith, no matter how much we want them to. The abundant life that Jesus came to give us results from denying our old self and choosing to live each moment in the sufficiency of who we are in him.

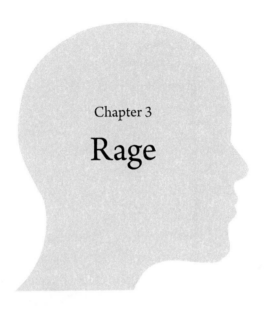

Chapter 3

Rage

*A hot-tempered man stirs up strife,
but the slow to anger calms a dispute.*
—Proverbs 15:18

The name on the patient list struck me as familiar. As I stood in the doorway of the waiting room of the hospital's psychiatry clinic, I realized that the name was that of a young man I had known in high school. The memories of those years came rushing back. Phil and I were on the basketball team together. He was the kind of kid everyone was afraid to be around because he was violent and unpredictable. He was a promising athlete until he was thrown off the basketball team for numerous fights during games; he had been expelled or suspended for fighting more times than I could count. Phil was banned from the local bowling alley for the same reason, and he was well known by the police in our small Texas town.

One incident in particular stood out to me, because it most clearly defined the nature of his anger. During lunch one day, Phil suddenly, and without warning, attacked his best friend for no apparent reason other than that he had become agitated during their conversation. There were no heated words, no insults, nothing that anyone could see as a reason for the attack.

Even I had been the target of Phil's anger on occasion. It was after one such incident that I made a statement that seemed to foreshadow my future profession. I said to some mutual friends, who were quite familiar with Phil's outbursts, "One day someone is going to find out he has a brain tumor or something." As I led Phil to the examination room for our interview, I wondered if I would be that person.

Because of Phil's problems with rage, his life since high school had been difficult. He had never completed college, had a long history of being unable to keep jobs, had been to see a number of mental health professionals with little success, and was alienated from his family and friends. His inability to control himself had left him depressed and alone. Phil had hit rock bottom. At the age of twenty-seven, he found himself at the psychiatry clinic; and in his mind, this was his last chance to get help. Fortunately, Phil was accepted into a rage treatment study we were conducting, and—thanks in large part to antiepileptic medication that helped control his impulsive aggressive outbursts—he finally received the help he so desperately needed.

Phil's problem isn't uncommon. I have heard this same story from literally hundreds of men and women during my career. Impulsive aggression, or rage, as it is more commonly referred to, has become a significant problem in our society. It is not just the behavior of criminals and the mentally ill, but is found close to home—in our families, in our friends, and, yes, even in our children. But there is the hope of the real possibility of change for those who struggle with this problem. And it is very much a struggle: a constant battle between control and rage, between the kind of person they see themselves as and the explosive personality that has destroyed their life and the lives of those around them.

IMPULSIVE AGGRESSION

Impulsive aggression is sudden, unpredictable, and extreme. It can vary in severity from a verbal outburst (yelling and screaming) to homicide. Following an outburst, individuals may describe a trigger or event that set them off. But their response was far beyond what would be considered normal or appropriate for the situation. These people often show genuine remorse and vow they will never do it again. The frequency of outbursts can vary from a few times a month to several times a day. Between outbursts they may appear normal and well controlled.

This is how impulsive aggression was described in a local radio advertisement I used to recruit participants for one of my research studies:

> This is an important announcement for men[1] who have trouble controlling their temper! Do you show your anger by throwing or breaking things? Do minor disagreements often turn into physical fights? Does this hair trigger cause you to overreact to minor insults and irritations? If your answer was yes to any of these questions, you may be eligible to participate in a study to test the effectiveness of a new treatment for rage outbursts. If you're a man whose family and friends have called you hotheaded or explosive or say that you have a short fuse, you may be eligible for this important study.

Does this sound like anyone you know? Unfortunately, rage is an all-too-common problem, and I would wager that everyone reading this book knows at least one person whom he or she would describe as "hotheaded or explosive."

PREVALENCE

How often does impulsive aggression occur? Crime statistics are commonly used to give us a general measure of the prevalence of violence in our society. For instance, approximately 1.8 million serious violent crimes, which include rape, robbery, aggravated assault, and homicide, are committed annually in the United States.[2] Sadly, it is also estimated that 1.3 million women are physically assaulted by an intimate partner every year.[3] The problem with using crime statistics such as these is that most impulsive aggression (e.g., road rage) is never reported to the criminal justice system. Thus, violent crime statistics are not that much help in giving us an idea of the prevalence of rage outbursts.

Having said that, three statistics are of interest in assessing the prevalence of this problem: (1) It is estimated that 30 percent of homicides result from an argument and are committed impulsively;[4] (2) the estimated number of individuals who meet diagnostic criteria for intermittent explosive disorder (IED), a psychiatric disorder in which rage outbursts are the core symptom, is thought to be no lower than 1.4 million annually;[5] and (3) surveys of "normal" individuals find that approximately 20 percent report having committed an impulsive aggressive act in the last six months.[6] These estimates suggest that rage is a very common problem that affects millions of individuals every year.

THE SCIENCE OF RAGE

Anger is a normal, God-given emotion. There is nothing inherently wrong or sinful about it. Jesus displayed righteous anger over sin during his earthly ministry (Mark 3:5; John 2:13–17), and we are called to do the same (Ephesians 4:26). Rage, however, which is anger expressed selfishly and without control, is clearly sinful (Galatians 5:19–21; James 1:19–20).

Within our brains there are specific areas that, when activated, can produce the emotional state we call anger, as well as related emotions such as fear and anxiety. To help regulate the expression of anger and these other emotions, God has given us highly sophisticated neural systems for threat detection and behavioral control. To say that anger has a physical basis is simply to recognize how God has created us. Remember, at one level we are biological creatures.

Brain Mechanisms

Problems in two areas of the brain, the prefrontal cortex (PFC) and the amygdala, are thought to produce a predisposition toward impulsive aggressive behavior. The PFC is a large area of the cortex located in the frontal lobe (directly behind your forehead). The cortex is the bumpy outer layer of the brain. Research has shown that the PFC is involved in attention, planning, organization, abstract reasoning, self-monitoring, and the ability to use feedback to change behavior.

The amygdala is a small mass of cells located deep within the temporal lobe (just above and in front of your ear, on both sides of your head). The amygdala is one of several structures within the brain that are part of what is called the limbic system. The primary functions of the limbic system are motivations (e.g., sexual drive) and emotions, particularly those related to survival. Several brain-imaging studies have shown that activity in the amygdala is increased in response to a direct threat and during negative emotional states such as fear and anger.[7]

The PFC and amygdala are physically connected through a pathway that allows them to communicate with each other. It is believed that the interaction between these two brain areas controls the intensity of our expressed anger. In a normal brain there is a strong relationship between the level of activity in the PFC and the amygdala. For instance, during a situation in which there is a direct threat (e.g., viewing angry faces), activity in both the PFC and the amygdala greatly increases. Increased activity in the amygdala results in fear and anger, while a synchronized increase in PFC activity appears to control how these negative emotions are expressed. In a sense, the PFC acts as the "brakes" for your brain, holding the angry impulses coming from the amygdala in check so that you can think of a more appropriate response to the perceived threat than a rage outburst (see Figure 4A). In other words, the PFC gives you a chance to think before you act on your anger.

A

B

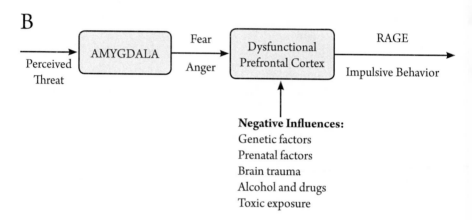

Figure 4. Overview of Aggressive Behavioral Control

In contrast, the impulsive aggressive individual has abnormally low activity in the PFC, which allows the angry impulses of an overactivated amygdala to go unrestrained.[8] Individuals with a dysfunctional PFC not only have problems with rage outbursts but generally behave impulsively, meaning that they tend to say and do things without regard to the consequences of their behavior (see Figure 4B). A brain without a fully functional PFC to constrain it is a dangerous thing, much like a speeding car without brakes.

A dysfunctional PFC can be acquired in a number of ways, including traumatic brain injury (TBI), infection, stroke, excessive alcohol and drug use, and toxic exposure. These insults to the brain can occur at any age and are capable of changing a once well-controlled and even-tempered individual into an explosive "Mr. Hyde" with a short fuse. PFC dysfunction is congenital in some individuals, resulting from problems in the prenatal environment (e.g., maternal alcohol use during pregnancy) or genetic influences.

Heritability

Through the years, one of the most common reasons people have given for participating in our impulsive aggression treatment studies has been, "I don't want my children to be like me." Sadly, in many instances the study participant's children were already showing serious problems with anger and aggression. Many of these same impulsive aggressive individuals have told me that their fathers and/or grandfathers also had problems controlling their anger. These two pieces of anecdotal evidence lead one to ask, Can rage be inherited—passed from parent to offspring genetically?

In animals, evidence for the heritability of aggressiveness is unquestioned. For instance, certain breeds of dogs have been selectively bred for enhanced dominance and aggression. Pit bulls and rottweilers currently receive the most public attention in this regard. Pit bulls have been banned in many locations because they are perceived as dangerous. The rottweiler traces its origins back to antiquity, probably descending from one of the ancient Roman droving dogs. Sources from the time indicate that these large, mastiff-like dogs accompanied the Roman legions on campaigns throughout Europe, driving and herding cattle as well as protecting the camps at night.

Can similar evidence for the heritability of aggressiveness be shown in humans? Obviously humans are not selectively bred like animals are, but there are two powerful methods for assessing the influence of heredity on specific traits in humans: twin studies and adoption studies. In a twin study, pairs of monozygotic (identical) and dizygotic (fraternal or nonidentical) twins are compared regarding a particular trait. Monozygotic twins have identical genotypes, meaning they have exactly the same genetic makeup. They also share the same environment growing up. In contrast, dizygotic twins, while sharing the same environment from birth, only have half of the same genes in common.

To conduct a twin study, scientists look for twin pairs in which one person shows a given trait, such as impulsive aggression, and then compare them. If both twins show the trait, they are said to be concordant. If only one twin shows the trait of interest, the pair is said to be discordant. Thus, if the trait is genetically influenced, the percentage of monozygotic (genetically identical) twins who are concordant for the trait should be higher than is the case with dizygotic twins. That is exactly what twin studies looking at impulsive aggression have found. Monozygotic twins show a significantly higher concordance rate for impulsive aggression compared to dizygotic twins, suggesting that genes do play a role in this behavior.[9]

Another way to estimate the heritability of impulsive aggression is to compare people who were adopted early in life with both their biological parents and their adoptive parents. If the aggressive behavior of the adoptee strongly resembles the aggressive behavior of one of their biological parents (who did not raise them), then it is probably influenced by genetic factors. If, instead, the adoptee's aggressive behavior resembles the aggressive behavior of one of their adoptive parents (who did raise them), then it is likely that environmental factors have a greater influence. Adoption studies looking at the heritability of aggression have shown varying results. Some studies have found impulsive aggressive behavior in both the adopted individual and one of his or her biological parents, suggesting a genetic influence, while other studies have found no such relationship.[10]

Taking both twin studies and adoption studies into consideration, it does appear that at least some aspect of rage is inherited (genetically influenced), although a complete explanation for the behavior most likely involves a complex interaction between genetic and environmental factors.

Neurochemistry

The human brain is composed of a complex mass of cells called neurons, which use both electrical current and chemical agents called neurotransmitters to send signals to one another. It is differing combinations of these signals that result in our thoughts, feelings, and behaviors. When the signals are disrupted or altered, abnormal thoughts and behaviors may result.

In the case of rage, disturbances in the neurotransmitter serotonin have been suggested to play a role. The serotonin system has been shown to control the activity of areas in the prefrontal cortex (PFC). Several studies have shown abnormal variations in the genes that code for the production of serotonin in individuals who display impulsive aggressive outbursts.[11] These rage-related genetic variations cause less serotonin to be made in the brain, which leads to reduced activity in the PFC and therefore results in the person having less ability to control his or her behavior. The consequence of low levels of serotonin in the brain is a spur-of-the-moment-style of living, in which aggression is one of many behaviors that are expressed impulsively.[12]

Intermittent Explosive Disorder

As mentioned earlier in this chapter, intermittent explosive disorder (IED) is a psychiatric disorder in which rage outbursts are the core symptom. IED is characterized by distinct impulsive aggressive outbursts that result in physical assault or the destruction of property.[13] The lifetime prevalence rate of IED is estimated to be approximately 7.3 percent of the population, with an average age of onset around fifteen years old. This disorder, like aggression in general, is more common in men than women.[14]

To be diagnosed with IED, an individual must meet the following three criteria: (1) Several separate episodes of failure to resist aggressive impulses have resulted in serious assaultive acts or destruction of property; (2) the degree of aggressiveness expressed during the episodes is grossly out of proportion to any precipitating psychosocial stressors; and (3) the aggressive episodes are not better accounted for by another mental disorder (e.g., psychotic disorder) and are not due to the direct effects of a substance (e.g., a drug of abuse) or a general medical condition (e.g., head injury). Given these restrictive criteria and the general subjectivity of psychiatric diagnosis, most individuals who display rage outbursts are never diagnosed with IED. To put IED in context, it is best thought of as only a small subset of all the individuals who display rage outbursts.

Treating Rage

There are two classes of medication that have been shown to be effective in treating impulsive aggressive individuals: selective serotonin reuptake inhibitors (SSRIs) and anticonvulsants. SSRIs like Prozac and Zoloft work specifically to increase the level of serotonin in the brain. A recent study of SSRIs in the treatment of impulsive aggressive patients found that taking Prozac for twelve weeks increased serotonin levels, normalized brain functioning, and significantly reduced aggression and irritability.[15]

Anticonvulsant medications like Dilantin and Tegretol are often used as mood-stabilizing agents in impulsive aggressive patients. The way anticonvulsants work in impulsive aggression, much like in epilepsy, seems to be through the control of neuron signaling. For a neuron (brain cell) to send a signal to another neuron, it must first reach a particular level of excitation or activation. You might say it needs to get charged up in order to fire. Anticonvulsant medications increase the level of excitation (charge) necessary for neurons to send signals to each other. This increased restraint on the ability of neurons to send signals causes activity across the brain to slow down, and the result is a general reduction of impulsive behavior.[16] It is important to remember that while pharmacotherapy is commonly used in the treatment of patients who display impulsive aggressive outbursts, no medication is presently approved by the Food and Drug Administration (FDA) specifically for such treatment.

Like many psychiatric problems, impulsive aggression is most effectively treated with a combination of medication and "talking" therapy, specifically cognitive behavioral therapy (CBT). In CBT, psychological and emotional problems are believed to be a result of the individual's negative thought patterns and behaviors. The major aim of the therapy is to help the person eliminate negative beliefs and/or behaviors and replace them with positive ones. Symptom reduction (e.g., fewer rage outbursts) is the goal of this type of therapy. Insight or understanding of the underlying cause of the problem is seen as either secondary or irrelevant. This approach is extremely directive, focusing on things that can be measured and observed (e.g., number of rage outbursts, reported mood), and avoids theoretical abstractions and speculations. Treatment usually lasts from twelve to twenty weeks. It may be conducted in a group setting, provided the people in the group have similar problems, or individually. As mentioned above, medication may be combined with CBT; and for many people, this is the best approach to treatment for rage outbursts.

Two Sides to Me

Melanie is a tall, strikingly beautiful eighteen-year-old woman whose attractive exterior hides a painful and traumatic past. Her mother divorced Melanie's physically abusive father when Melanie was only two years old. Her father continued to abuse her physically when she would visit him, culminating with him striking Melanie's face so hard that he broke her nose when she was fifteen. Soon after the divorce, Melanie's mother married a man who began sexually abusing her when she was seven. The sexual abuse went on for several years.

As a way of escape, Melanie started using alcohol and drugs at the age of eight. She also started cutting herself and burning herself with cigarettes. Not surprisingly, Melanie became a discipline problem at school; and she dropped out of tenth grade and began living on her own.

I first met Melanie when she was referred to me for a psychological assessment by a local mental health clinic where she had gone to seek help for uncontrollable rage outbursts. She said, "There are two sides to me; my mood can change in an instant." In her short lifetime, Melanie had been involved in numerous fights and assaults. She described several episodes in which she had attacked and choked her roommate. On another occasion, while Melanie was driving, she and a friend began to argue. Melanie pulled the car over and ordered her friend to get out. When her friend refused, Melanie attempted to push her out the door and then stepped on the accelerator pedal. Hanging out of the open car door but with the seat belt still buckled, her friend struck the pavement several times and was seriously injured. This incident scared Melanie so much that she decided to get help.

In addition to her history of physical/sexual abuse, substance use, and self-harm, Melanie also reported to me symptoms consistent with an eating disorder (bulimia nervosa) and showed signs of a significant clinical depression. Neuropsychological assessment of her cognitive function showed a mild right frontal-lobe dysfunction. Clinically, she met the diagnostic criteria for major depressive disorder and borderline personality disorder.[17]

Melanie had every one of the biological predispositions for rage described above. She inherited the genes of a violent and abusive father, her frontal cortex was mildly impaired, and she showed psychiatric problems (self-harm, depression, bulimia) consistent with a dysfunction in the serotonin system of her brain. This is not to mention a history of traumatic physical and sexual abuse, which by itself could lead to problems with behavioral control and aggression. The fact that she was currently employed and was pursuing a general equivalency diploma (GED) spoke to her amazing resilience. Biologically, Melanie never had a chance. But she wanted to change, and it was that motivation to overcome her past that set her on the road to recovery.

FOOLISH ANGER

The topic of uncontrolled anger is common throughout the Bible. One needs to look no further than the Wisdom Books to find a detailed description of the rageful person and the dire consequences of this sinful behavior. These verses describe the impulsive aggressive individual as a "fool." In the Scriptures, foolishness is often contrasted with wisdom. The "fool" is one who is self-sufficient and does not truly know God (Psalm 14:1; Proverbs 1:7), while the "wise" person is dependent on God and knows

Selected Verses from the Wisdom Books
Concerning Uncontrolled Anger

Job
"Anger slays the foolish man, and jealousy kills the simple" (5:2).

Psalms
"Cease from anger and forsake wrath; do not fret; it leads only to evildoing" (37:8).

Proverbs
"A fool's anger is known at once, but a prudent man conceals dishonor" (12:16).

"A quick-tempered man acts foolishly, and a man of evil devices is hated" (14:17).

"He who is slow to anger has great understanding, but he who is quick-tempered exalts folly" (14:29).

"A hot-tempered man stirs up strife, but the slow to anger calms a dispute" (15:18).

"Do not associate with a man given to anger; or go with a hot-tempered man, or you will learn his ways and find a snare for yourself" (22:24–25).

"Like a city that is broken into and without walls is a man who has no control over his spirit" (25:28).

"A fool always loses his temper, but a wise man holds it back" (29:11).

"An angry man stirs up strife, and a hot-tempered man abounds in transgression" (29:22).

Ecclesiastes
"Do not be eager in your heart to be angry, for anger resides in the bosom of fools" (7:9).

him intimately (Job 28:28; Psalm 111:10; Proverbs 9:10). The explosive individual is described as one who has no honor, is hated by others, exalts sin, and causes harm to all those he encounters. Ultimately, uncontrolled anger leads to death, both spiritually and physically.

We feel anger when we perceive an injustice or see evil. God's purpose for human anger is "to motivate us to take positive, loving action . . . to set the wrong right."[18] Human anger was created in the image of God's anger (Genesis 1:26). As author Gary Chapman wrote, "When God sees evil, He experiences anger. Anger is His logical response to injustice or unrighteousness."[19] God's righteous anger is an overt expression of his holiness and justice, which are attributes of his glory. Righteous anger is slow to develop (Psalm 86:15, 103:8, 145:8; Joel 2:13; Jonah 4:2; Nahum 1:3), fully controlled (Psalm 78:38, 85:3), limited in duration (Psalm 30:5; Micah 7:18), and always fulfills its intended purpose, which is transformation (Job 42:7–9).

Human anger, while originally created in the image of God's anger, has been tainted by sin. Rather than expressing righteous anger toward injustice and evil, we display anger when we believe that our selfish wants and desires are not being fully satisfied. This is the definition of "the flesh": selfishly trying to meet our wants and desires rather than depending on God for our provision. Add to this a lack of behavioral control (possibly resulting from a brain dysfunction), and you have an individual who lives at the mercy of his or her fleshly feelings and emotions (Galatians 5:19–21). Feel angry—explode! Feel anxious—blow up! Feel fearful—lash out!

Rage, then, is the exact opposite of godly, righteous anger. It develops quickly, is uncontrolled, lacks purpose, and, because of its selfish nature, results in long-lasting fear and anxiety.

LIVING WITH RAGE

I first met Robert in January 1999. He responded to a radio ad, much like the one cited earlier in this chapter, that I was using to recruit men with temper-control problems for a study. The study's goal was to test the effectiveness of the anticonvulsant Dilantin in the treatment of rage outbursts. Robert, fifty-seven years old at the time, was a successful general contractor. He had been married to his wife Cindy for twenty-five years. This was a second marriage for both of them. Robert had two children from his first marriage and two stepchildren from Cindy's previous marriage.

Sitting in my office, one of the first things Robert said to me was, "God sent me to you." He described his lifelong problem with uncontrolled anger. He told me that his father, who also had a temper-control problem, physically abused him as a child. Robert's rage outbursts usually involved yelling and screaming, along with throwing and/or breaking things and punching walls. He described himself as very organized and a "black-and-white thinker," intolerant of unexpected change and easily frustrated by "the stupidity and inefficiencies of others."

Robert estimated that he had, on average, four rage outbursts a month. He was very embarrassed by these outbursts, describing them as "child-ish." He felt they were an indication of a weakness in his character. He said he was attempting to control his temper, at the time, through prayer but acknowledged that he had been unable to change on his own.

The most recent outburst had occurred two weeks earlier. Robert and Cindy had been arguing when he suddenly lost control, destroyed the hair dryer she was using, and punched a hole in the bathroom wall near her head. He admitted that in the past he had grabbed and shoved Cindy during arguments but denied doing anything more. He felt that he had "abused" Cindy, "but not to where it was illegal."

Cindy told me that she had sought counsel from the elders of their church in the past when Robert had become physical with her. After several meetings followed by Robert's failure to control his aggression, the elders had given him an ultimatum: "Stop being physically abusive toward your wife, or you will be put outside the fellowship of the church."

In my initial neuropsychological assessment, I found Robert to be highly impulsive. He did not meet the criteria for the diagnosis of any psychiatric disorder, but his testing did indicate a mild prefrontal cortex dysfunction. In my research I have found that impulsive aggressive men often use alcohol or marijuana to try to level out their moods and control their rage outbursts. Robert was not using alcohol, but he did admit that he smoked marijuana at least once a month. Robert met all the study criteria and was accepted into the anticonvulsant study.

Robert successfully completed the twelve weeks of the study. During the six weeks that he was taking a placebo (a sugar pill), Cindy reported that he had four impulsive aggressive outbursts—which was consistent with Robert's prestudy estimate for the frequency of his rage outbursts. During the six weeks that he was taking Dilantin, Robert had no impulsive aggressive outbursts. At my final meeting with them, Cindy tearfully stated, "This study has saved our marriage." Robert said, "I now have my life back." I sent a report of Robert's results to his primary care physician and referred him to a local Christian counselor.

Five years later, I spoke with Robert about his experience in the study and about his progress since then. He was still taking Dilantin daily, he had successfully completed his sessions with the Christian counselor, and he had not had an impulsive aggressive outburst in over a year.

MINISTERING TO THOSE WITH UNCONTROLLED ANGER

What I have been describing as rage or impulsive aggression is a chronic problem that people can struggle with for many years. Anyone is capable of displaying a single episode of rage, but what I am describing here is a long-term problem with self-control. As the body of Christ, how are we to respond to those individuals within our faith communities who, like Robert, show chronic temper-control problems?

First, family members and anyone else in the path of the impulsive aggressor must be protected. I have sat across an interview table from far too many men and women who have attempted to minimize their spouse's violence by blaming themselves. In Robert's case, the leaders of his church were trying to protect the family, but I believe they waited too long. In my opinion, after the first physically aggressive act, the family should temporarily leave the home until the person seeks real help. The mistake is waiting and allowing the aggression to escalate. It is important to remember that a single impulsive aggressive outburst can be deadly.

Second, we must learn to hold the explosive person accountable for his or her destructive response to anger. Fits of rage are sinful works of the flesh (Galatians 5:19–21) that grieve the very heart of God (Ephesians 4:29–32). The common response to a rage outburst is to back down and avoid the circumstance or topic that triggered the incident. People usually walk on eggshells around the rageful, so the problem is never dealt with or brought into the light. Rage is not solely biological; there is clearly a learned component. The avoid-at-all-costs response actually reinforces the idea that having a rage outburst is an effective way to get what you want—like rewarding a two-year-old's temper tantrum. The impulsive aggressive individual must be held accountable for his or her actions either by the family, the church, or the criminal justice system.

Finally, the focus of pastoral ministry toward those struggling with rage should be the sufficiency of Christ. Remember, sinful anger is an attempt to get our fleshly wants and desires fulfilled. Once people come to the end of their own self-sufficiency and recognize that they are a new creation in Christ (2 Corinthians 5:17), fleshly desires become easier to identify and control. As they submit to the indwelling Spirit for the renewing of their minds (Romans 12:2), sinful behaviors begin to change. They must be taught the proper way to deal with frustration and stress (James 1:19–20), because exploding in anger is the only option they presently know. Godly fellow believers, walking alongside them and holding them accountable for their actions, can help bring about an amazing transformation.

Having spiritual and biological components, there is no quick fix for impulsive aggression. Robert had been struggling with rage for most of his fifty-seven years. Pharmacological treatment in conjunction with pastoral counseling was necessary in his journey to wholeness. But for those who presently feel trapped in a nightmare of rage and violence, let me say this: Through Christ, real change is possible. I have seen it happen!

Chapter 4

Lust and Adultery

You shall not commit adultery.
—Exodus 20:14

"I never would have thought it could happen to me, but looking back now I see that I was on the road to adultery for years before it actually occurred."

Tim is a successful man, an executive at a large pharmaceutical company. He and his wife, Sarah, have been married for over twenty years and have three children. What most people don't know is that this beautiful family picture was almost destroyed by a seven-year adulterous affair that Tim had with a female coworker.

"I always saw women as a conquest, even back in high school." Highly promiscuous in college, Tim told me that he was unfaithful to Sarah from when he first started dating her. "I didn't think much of it. We were in college, and I wanted to have fun."

Married soon after graduation, Tim constantly struggled with sexual fantasies and lust. Occasionally he would use pornography to soothe his dissatisfaction with his and Sarah's sex life. Sexual fantasizing and masturbation became a daily ritual. "I was really living two lives. My home life was church and family, but in my mind I was fantasizing about sex with every woman I saw."

Tim also admitted that he loved to flirt. "It made me feel like at least someone found me attractive." Tim's flirtations were often playfully reciprocated, but nothing more ever came of them until Bridget was hired for a job in Tim's office under his supervision. Bridget was different from the other women with whom Tim flirted. She was young, single, and very interested in his advances.

"I knew it was going to happen before we ever went on the business trip together. I guess in my mind I had actually planned it out. One part of me wanted it to happen." Thus began an adulterous relationship that would almost end Tim's marriage. "While I loved the sex, the guilt was so heavy and intense that there were days I almost couldn't function. I started having panic attacks."

Tim tried to end the affair several times but would find himself running back to Bridget every time he felt Sarah wasn't showing him enough attention. "I was just selfish. What about my wife, my children? I also wasn't thinking about Bridget. She didn't deserve to be used like that either. Even though I was fully responsible for my behavior, I felt trapped."

After seven years of secret phone calls, private e-mails, and clandestine rendezvous, Sarah finally found out about Tim and Bridget's relationship. "She should have left me, but thank God she didn't. Her faith was so much stronger than mine. Christ sustained her through that difficult time and allowed me an opportunity to earn her trust again."

DEFINING THE PROBLEM

The word "adultery" isn't used that often anymore. Laden with moral and religious association, the word seems old and out of date. It brings to most peoples' minds Moses and the Ten Commandments or Hester Prynne of Hawthorne's classic, *The Scarlet Letter*. In our modern society, we are more likely to use terms that are judgmentally neutral—like "extra-marital sex"—to describe this sinful act. We say, "She was having a fling," "He was fooling around," or "They had a thing." Somehow that doesn't seem so harsh or critical. After all, it was just a little indiscretion. This is far from the Old Testament's severe view of adultery, which called for both the man and the woman involved to be put to death (Leviticus 20:10).

The biblical view of adultery does not necessarily refer to the actual sexual act but pertains primarily to the breaking of a covenantal relationship. For instance, the Hebrew word *na'aph*, which is translated "adultery," is probably better translated "break wedlock."[1] In the Old Testament, this word is also often used figuratively to describe when the people of Israel turned to idolatry and the worship of other gods. Having broken their covenant with God, they are said to have committed "spiritual" adultery (e.g., Jeremiah 5:7; Ezekiel 23:37; Hosea 4:12).

Similarly, in the New Testament, the Greek word *moicheuo*, translated "adultery," is used in this spiritual sense to describe the first-century Jewish people (Matthew 12:39; Mark 8:38), apostate believers in the early church (James 4:4), and false teachers (2 Peter 2:14). In the Sermon on the Mount, Jesus emphasized this broader view of adultery as a sin of covenant breaking: "You have heard that it was said, 'You shall not commit adultery'; but I say to you that everyone who looks at a woman with lust for her has already committed adultery with her in his heart" (Matthew 5:27–28). Understood in this way, adultery does not have to involve actual sex or even another person. It becomes more of an attitude than an act. A husband looking at pornography and a wife involved in a secret emotional relationship via the Internet have both violated their marital covenants and committed adultery.

What about lust in the mind of a single person? Is that sin? It is important to remember that any desire to sin is sin (Matthew 5:27–28; James
1:14–15). Lust is a sin of wrong desire. It is not lust for a single person
to want to have sex. That is the way God made us. What is wrong is to
want the pleasure of sex without the commitment of marriage. The New
Testament uses the word *porneia* to describe this type of sin. In English,
this is traditionally translated "fornication" or "sexual immorality" (Mark
7:21; Galatians 5:19). Ironically, it is this Greek word *porneia* that serves
as the root for our English word "pornography." The use of pornographic
material may be our best measure of how often the sin of lust occurs.

PREVALENCE

It is impossible to pick up a newspaper or magazine, watch television,
or log onto the Internet without being exposed to highly sexual entertain-
ment and/or advertisements. Images used in marketing today would have
been considered pornographic by the average person just a generation
ago. The pornography industry, which includes Internet sites, videos,
magazines, cable TV, and strip clubs, generates approximately $13 billion
dollars in annual revenue in the United States. Worldwide, pornography
revenue estimates exceed $90 billion dollars per year.[2]

Every second, 28,258 Internet users are viewing pornography. This is
not just a problem for men; one out of every three visitors to pornographic
Internet sites is a woman. Seventy percent of these women report that they
keep their online activities a secret, and 17 percent report struggling with a
sexual addiction. Perhaps the most troubling part of this is how vulnerable
Internet access has made our children. The average age of first Internet pornography exposure is eleven, and 80 percent of fifteen- to seventeen-year-
olds report having had multiple exposures to hard-core pornography.[3]

This societal preoccupation with sex has also had a detrimental effect
on marriages. Surveys in the United States find that sexual infidelity occurs
in slightly less than 25 percent of couples over the course of a marriage,
with more men than women engaging in adultery.[4] In a global survey of

sexual attitudes and behaviors in 300,000 participants across forty-one countries, 22 percent of married individuals reported having been involved in an extramarital affair.[5] We live in a highly sexualized era. Young children are increasingly exposed to graphic sexual material, and attitudes and beliefs about sexuality are shaped by the ever-increasing influence of the pornography industry. These are truly troubling times.

THE SCIENCE OF SEX

"Be fruitful and multiply" (Genesis 1:28). This was the first command God gave to human beings. You might say, in a sense, that we were created to mate. God made us male and female so that each one of us might find a companion (Genesis 2:18) with whom we could raise a family.[6]

In the animal kingdom, only 3 percent of mammalian species form a long-term attachment to a mating partner.[7] In humans, however, monogamous marriage occurs in all contemporary societies and is clearly the predominant mating approach.[8] Monogamous relationships are part of God's plan for us, so much so that he created within each of us a set of specific biological systems to guide the process. One system draws us toward the opposite sex, while another makes us want to select a particular mate and form a family. Once we have children, a third system encourages us to stay together and raise those children. Let's look at each of these systems individually.

Sexual Motivation System

The purpose of this system is to motivate us to seek a sexual union. This strong motivational tendency or instinct is often called our sex drive. It is a physiological need for sexual activity, a craving for sexual gratification. The drive is relatively constant for a male, while a female's drive is more periodic. This system becomes activated at puberty, when two structures in the brain, the hypothalamus and the anterior pituitary gland, cause the gonads (testes in the male, ovaries in the female) to release steroid sex hormones. In males, these hormones are called

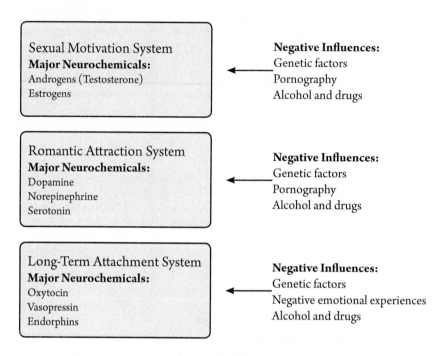

Figure 5. Overview of Sexual-Relational Motivation Systems

androgens, of which testosterone is the most important. In females, the ovaries release estrogens. When androgens and estrogens become active in our bodies for the first time, they generate sexual desire—not a sinful desire, but a God-given drive to seek out and be near members of the opposite sex for the ultimate purpose of finding a mate. Steroid sex hormones are also responsible for sexual maturation, shaping our bodies into adult men and women.

Our sex drive is rather nonspecific; if it had a motto, it would be "Anyone will do." For example, testosterone increases in a man when he is simply in close proximity to a woman, whether or not he finds her attractive. This hormonal increase motivates males to pursue females for the purposes of mating. In women, estrogen governs what might be called the receptive sex drive and makes her responsive to the man stimulated by testosterone to pursue her.[9]

Androgens and estrogens drive us together, but they don't mediate the formation of emotional bonds. A second biological system is responsible for mate selection, or what might better be called "falling in love."

Romantic Attraction System

If you have ever been in a serious relationship, you know the symptoms: lightheadedness, upset stomach, loss of appetite, confusion, insomnia, obsessive thoughts, and abnormally elevated mood. It's not a new psychiatric disorder—it's love! While the sexual motivation system drives us toward the opposite sex, the romantic attraction system enables us to focus our mating efforts on a preferred individual: Mr. or Ms. Right. Many factors, such as timing, health, finances, childhood experiences, and cultural forces play a role in triggering to whom one becomes attracted. Once all these factors are realized in a particular individual, the romantic attraction system takes over.

The primary neurochemicals in this system are dopamine, norepinephrine, and serotonin. Dopamine could be referred to as the "pleasure chemical." When released in the brain, it produces a feeling of ecstasy and bliss. Dopamine is most active in the areas of the brain related to reward and pleasure, the same areas involved in addiction; and that is why high levels of dopamine bring about a chemical rush similar to the effects of amphetamines. Norepinephrine is chemically related to adrenalin and when released in the brain causes a state of heightened excitement and focused attention. Serotonin is predominately an inhibitory neurochemical and is suppressed by dopamine activity. This means that when dopamine levels are high, serotonin levels are low. Low levels of serotonin in the brain bring about feelings of euphoria and obsessional thinking.

Here is how the romantic attraction system works. When a potential mate who meets all the necessary attraction criteria is found, the romantic attraction system causes dopamine and norepinephrine to be released in the brain. This flood of neurochemicals brings about a pleasurable feeling, heightened excitement, and focused attention. Increasing dopamine activity causes serotonin levels in the brain to drop, resulting in feelings of euphoria and obsessional thoughts (i.e., an inability to stop thinking about the person). This type of neural activation is perceived as very pleasurable, causing the individual to want to be near this special person again and again. In fact, the mere thought of that person brings about a similar rush of pleasurable neurochemicals. Your brain has you hooked: you simply can't get enough of that person because, in a very real sense, you're addicted.

Two recent brain-imaging studies of people deeply in love found that, when viewing a picture of their beloved, blood flow significantly increased in areas of the brain known to be involved in reward and craving, and it decreased in areas related to negative emotions such as sadness and fear.[10] In other words, the brains of people deeply in love don't look like those of people experiencing strong emotions or sexual arousal—but instead like those of people using cocaine! This makes sense, biologically, since the romantic attraction system uses the same neural mechanisms that are activated during the process of addiction.

Given this extreme change in brain chemistry during the initial phases of romantic attraction, what happens if the relationship doesn't work out? Much like a drug addict unable to get a fix, the romantic who is deprived of the lover goes into neurochemical withdrawal, as dopamine and norepinephrine levels in the brain plummet and serotonin levels rise. This leads to sluggishness, dejection, and depression.[11]

But let's imagine that this hypothetical relationship continues to mature. How does the brain move from a lovesick infatuation to a committed, lifelong, monogamous relationship?

Long-Term Attachment System

Despite how discouraging the situation may appear—with rampant promiscuity, a divorce rate of 50 percent, and increasing numbers of children born to single mothers—we were each created to be in a committed monogamous relationship that would last a lifetime. The third biological system involved in human pair bonding we will call the long-term attachment system. This system takes us from romantic attraction to deep emotional commitment.

The primary neurochemicals at work in this system are oxytocin, vasopressin, and endorphins (the body's natural painkillers). Oxytocin is also known as the "cuddle hormone." It promotes uterine contractions during childbirth, milk production during nursing, and is involved in infant-mother bonding. In both men and women, oxytocin is released in the brain during positive emotions and physical contact such as massage, hand-holding, or hugging. Increasing levels of oxytocin bring about feelings of security, care, and comfort. For example, oxytocin levels surge when a new father holds his infant child. During orgasm, the brain releases oxytocin in women and vasopressin (a neurochemical closely related to oxytocin) in men, promoting sexual pleasure and emotional bonding. Endorphins are also released in the brain during sex and produce a general sense of well-being, causing a person to feel soothed, peaceful, and secure.

So how do we move from infatuation to attachment? Drunk on pleasurable neurochemicals (dopamine and norepinephrine), the couple newly in love begins to become more intimate—touching, kissing, hugging, holding hands—causing oxytocin levels to rise in their brains. This brings about feelings of security, care, and comfort. Oxytocin and vasopressin (released from the hypothalamus) interfere with the dopamine and norepinephrine pathways of the romantic attraction system, which explains why passionate love gradually fades as attachment grows. When the couple begin to have sex, dopamine is released in the brain's reward center, making the experience enjoyable and ensuring that they want to do it again. Because oxytocin, vasopressin, and endorphin levels also rise during this intimate experience, they also want to have sex with the same person again because that will bring feelings of well-being, peace, and security. In fact, research suggests that the more sex they have, the greater their emotional bond will be.[12]

High levels of oxytocin and vasopressin decrease testosterone levels in the male, minimizing the pull of the sexual motivation system to seek out other potential mates. Testosterone levels plunge even further once the couple's first infant is born. The suppressing effects of oxytocin on the sexual motivation system may also help explain why women report a decline in their sex drive after childbirth.

Compared to the other phases, the attachment stage continues for the longest time and has to be strong enough to withstand the many problems and distractions that come during a lifetime together. While these three motivational systems strongly influence our behavior toward members of the opposite sex, we are not blindly controlled by them.

Prefrontal Cortex

In the last chapter, I described the prefrontal cortex (PFC) as the "brakes" of your brain. While the PFC is involved in a number of higher cognitive processes—including attention, planning, organization, abstract reasoning, and self-monitoring—the most important in the context of lust and adultery is what we refer to as social control. This is the ability to suppress emotional or sexual urges that, if left unchecked, could lead to socially unacceptable outcomes. So while our behaviors may be strongly influenced neurochemically, as described above, the behaviors we display are ultimately the result of our own reason and choice.

HOW BIOLOGY CAN CAUSE RELATIONSHIPS TO FAIL

Now let's look at problems and events that can adversely affect this process. The first difficulty results from the fact that the motivational systems I have just described function independently of one another. While the slow progression from desire to attraction to attachment is what God may have intended, the independence of the three systems also makes the following possible: an individual can have sex with someone they are not romantically attracted to; at the same time, that individual can also be romantically attracted to a second person with whom they have never had sex; and that same individual can also be emotionally attached to a third person for whom they feel no sexual desire or romantic attraction. Anthropologist

Helen Fisher, a leading researcher in the area of romantic love, has said that "the neural independence of [these systems] undoubtedly contributes to contemporary worldwide patterns of adultery and divorce."[13] While it is unclear whether the independence of these systems is a consequence of humanity's fall or just poor control by the prefrontal cortex, the end result is still sin.

A second way in which problems can occur in this process is through individual differences in the various neurochemicals necessary for relational success. For instance, research has shown that a man's baseline level of testosterone is influenced by genetic factors.[14] In other words, it is inherited. While most men show normal baseline levels of testosterone, some men are born with abnormally low levels, while others have very high baseline levels. Studies have shown that men with high baseline levels of testosterone are more likely to leave the home because of troubled marital relations, extramarital sex, or spousal abuse.[15] In fact, baseline testosterone level and marital satisfaction have been shown to have an inverse relationship. This means that high baseline levels of testosterone result in less marital satisfaction.

Neurochemical levels can also be affected by environmental events. Janice Crouse, senior fellow at Concerned Women for America, has reported on research that found "the production of oxytocin varied among women according to the level of distress and anxiety or the degree of security in their relationships. The women who had fewer negative emotional relationships in their lifetime experienced greater oxytocin production."[16] These results suggest that women with a significant history of relational issues are less able to form significant emotional bonds with subsequent partners because of low oxytocin production.

These are just two examples, but clearly genetic and environmental factors can have significant adverse effects on neurochemical levels that influence an individual's future romantic relationships.

The third way in which these motivational systems are adversely affected is through drug abuse. The misuse of substances such as alcohol, marijuana, and cocaine has significant adverse effects on neurochemical levels in the body. Excessive alcohol use has been shown to lower oxytocin and vasopressin levels, which compromise an individual's ability to bond emotionally. Marijuana use lowers testosterone levels, affecting sexual drive, and cocaine stimulates the dopamine-driven reward system to such an extreme level that relationships and sexual experiences perceived as enjoyable in the past are no longer satisfying.

Another way in which the relational systems can be abused is through misuse of the systems themselves, specifically through the use of pornography. Viewing pornography significantly increases testosterone levels in both men and women.[17] In addition, if individuals sexually gratify themselves while looking at pornography, their dopamine-rich attraction system is activated, and the experience is highly rewarding. Pornography gives both men and women a very strong chemical rush and alters the way they think about sex. Through frequent use, people become sexually attached to pornographic material and have trouble getting the same kind of satisfaction from sex in a normal relationship. Addiction counselor Robert Ellis describes it this way: "Pornography lures the flesh into doing what it does best—pervert a normally pleasurable and pure instinct (sex) into a lust-filled, sin-laden, chemically-driven compulsion."[18]

BIOLOGICAL DESIGN REFLECTED IN THE SCRIPTURES

As a scientist, it never ceases to amaze me just how accurate and complete the Scriptures are in their description of natural phenomena. The neurobiological processes related to attraction and attachment outlined above can clearly be seen in verses discussing marriage and adultery throughout the Bible. For instance, the sex drive is seen as a God-given biological instinct that must be controlled in order to avoid sin (1 Corinthians 7:5, 9; 1 Thessalonians 4:3–5).

Descriptions of this sex drive as causing an individual to "burn with passion" or have "lustful passion" appear to be rather colorful metaphors for surging sex hormone levels. The marital relationship is seen as the only place that this drive can be brought under control and expressed in a godly manner (Proverbs 5:15–20; 1 Corinthians 7:1–5; Hebrews 13:4).

The Scriptures also suggest that a sexual relationship physically alters a couple in such a way that they become "one flesh" (Genesis 2:24; Matthew 19:4–6; 1 Corinthians 6:16). This reference can be understood and explained by increased levels of oxytocin and vasopressin in the brain that bring about emotional bonding. When a sexual relationship is sinful (such as in adultery or fornication), the Scriptures imply that the adverse effects can be both physical and long-term; Paul writes that sexually immoral practices such as these cause people to sin against their own bodies (1 Corinthians 6:18). I believe this references neurochemical changes that occur during the act of adultery or fornication, altering a person's brain in such a way that his or her other intimate relationships (present or future) are damaged. We have been spiritually transformed in Christ, but sin still has a physical stranglehold on our bodies (Romans 7:22–25). It is only through the power of the indwelling Spirit that sin can be mastered (Genesis 4:7).

LIFE AFTER SEXUAL ADDICTION

Mark grew up in a Christian home. He made a decision to follow Christ early in his life, and he was baptized at the age of six on Christmas Day. That same year his mother was diagnosed with a rare neurological disorder, marking the beginning of a difficult eight-year journey of hospitalizations and dangerous experimental treatments. Mark estimates that his mother was in the hospital 75 percent of the time during those eight years. Mark's father, the local high school principal, was under tremendous stress as he struggled to take care of Mark and his two older sisters. While a loving father, he was not emotionally close to his children.

At the age of ten, Mark had an experience that would forever change his life. As he had many times before, Mark went to play at his friend's house. The boys' families went to church together, and Mark often went to their house. This particular afternoon, Mark's friend wanted to show him something that he had hidden in the field next door: a *Playboy* magazine. It seems that this boy had found his two older brothers' stash of pornographic magazines and taken a few for himself. Mark really didn't know what to make of the magazine, but he found the pictures strangely enticing. Looking at pornography became a regular event every time Mark went to this boy's house.

As Mark entered high school, and puberty, he was given a television with cable access to watch in his bedroom. A sick mother and a stressed-out father made for a difficult home life. The couple often fought, and Mark was regularly left unsupervised. He began to seek out a source of emotional comfort, which he found late at night from adult movies broadcast on cable. Soon Mark began to gratify himself sexually while watching the movies, and this behavior continued regularly throughout his high school years.

After graduating from high school, Mark began attending a Christian college. It was during his freshman year that another college student opened his eyes to the sinful sexual behavior that had taken control of him. Mark found that his constant sexual fantasizing, use of pornography, and subsequent masturbation had made him isolated and inhibited toward women. Once challenged by his college friend to stop his sinful behavior, Mark tried to remove the influence of pornography from his life. This resulted in several years of temporary successes followed inevitably by frustrating failures.

Still struggling with lust, Mark began serving as a youth ministry intern during his junior year of college. The next year he became the interim youth director, which led to a full-time ministry position immediately after graduation. All the while, Mark was struggling to control his lust and use of pornography. After several years at the church, Mark felt led to leave his youth ministry position and attend seminary. Now unchecked by a ministry position, Mark was introduced to the Internet, and his use of pornography began to increase dramatically. He was hooked—a seminary student addicted to pornography.

Lust and Adultery   59

Mark told me that he never really felt convicted about his sin until he started to be intentional about spending time with God every day. Through Mark's daily time with the Lord, God began to work in Mark's heart. Initially the process was much the same as it had been. He would try to remove the temptation from his life (for example, canceling Internet access), only to quickly fail and find himself right back where he had started. Mark's journey to freedom began when he started to get real accountability from men who had been set free from sexual addictions themselves. These men reminded him of two simple truths: "God loves you and wants to care for you," and "Lust does not have power over you anymore." Mark finally began to have real seasons of freedom that would last for months, even years. When he was tempted or failed, he would confess it to God and his accountability partners and move forward.

A few years later, Mark began dating and eventually became engaged to a young woman named Jocelyn. Prior to their wedding, Mark told Jocelyn about his past problems with pornography. One year into their marriage he struggled again, but again he surrendered his addiction to the Lord and made it through. That was seven years ago. Mark is still on the journey. A full-time pastor, he has set high boundaries for himself and has strong accountability with other men. Keeping his past sins in the light has made all the difference. Mark now ministers to men who struggle with lust, and he and Jocelyn are passionate about helping young couples build strong marriages.

Mark said to me, "Now I'm pursuing Jesus as my heart's delight. He is satisfying, and it's to him I go for comfort now."

MINISTERING TO THOSE WHO STRUGGLE WITH LUST AND ADULTERY

We were created for relationship with one another (Genesis 2:18). God made us male and female so that we might be involved in the creative process of reproduction through physical intimacy. He designed within each of us a set of biological systems that prompt us to seek out a companion and form long-term emotional connections. Unfortunately, our bodies have been scarred by original sin, and we live in a fallen world. Our sinful state has resulted in an epidemic of problems related to lust. People like Tim, who are dissatisfied with their lives and seek fulfillment through adulterous sexual relationships, and people like Mark, who seek comfort and control through sexual fantasies and self-gratification, find that sexual sin comes at the expense of real intimacy.

All men (and many women) struggle with lust. Our "feel good" culture tells us to follow our primal impulses with little thought of the consequences. Stephen Arterburn describes it this way: "Our society helps condition us toward addictive sex. The media have helped make the unusual appear to be normal. Multiple sex partners, repeated affairs, sex on every first date: these behaviors no longer shock the regular viewer of primetime television. Many who grow up in such an environment will be predisposed to sex addiction."[19] The sinful culture we live in takes our normal, God-given biological drives and turns them against us.

How might we minister to those who are struggling with lust or are involved in an adulterous affair? First, we must all understand that the power for real-life transformation rests only in Christ. Change is not possible when individuals have no fear of God or of the consequences of their sin. An encounter with the living God that brings conviction of sin is the first step toward freedom. Point them to Christ; he is the agent of change. If their "private" sins have been exposed, help them recognize that this is the mercy of God being manifested in their life. By bringing their sin into the light, God has given them an opportunity to be truly free.

Second, continually remind them of these two biblical truths: (1) God loves you and has a purpose and plan for your life (Jeremiah 29:11); and (2) because you are a new creation in Christ, sin no longer has power over you (Romans 6:6; 2 Corinthians 5:17; Galatians 2:20). They must understand that the unconditional love and acceptance they have sought through sex can only be found in God. Similarly, the feeling that they are controlled by their sexual impulses is a deceptive illusion. In Christ, they have a choice: either they will set their mind on the things of the Spirit, or they will choose to follow their fleshly desires (Romans 8:5–6). These truths are the foundation for the journey to freedom before them.

Help them learn to delight in God. Encourage them to spend time with the Lord every day through study of the Scriptures, prayer, worship, or just listening to his guiding Spirit. Their concept of normal sexual intimacy has been significantly altered by their sinful behavior, and because of this their minds must be retrained (Romans 12:1–2). The biological systems God originally intended to draw them into a lifelong monogamous relationship have been wrongly focused and must be redirected. Begin that process by showing them that relational as well as sexual satisfaction is based in their relationship with Christ (Ephesians 5:25–32).

Finally, it is very important that from this point forward that they "walk in the Light" (1 John 1:7). Encourage them to find a group of men or women (men with men; women with women) to whom they can be truly accountable—not a vague, surface level of accountability, but full disclosure and confession. They need someone they can call when they are tempted, someone they can confess to when they fall short. Similar to an alcoholic who has left drinking behind, they must recognize their past weakness and be intentional about their future behavior. Help them set appropriate boundaries in relation to Internet access, cell phone use, business travel, etc.

Spiritual and biological hurdles must be overcome in the journey to freedom from sexual sin. Fortunately, the God we serve has overcome the world (John 16:33; 1 John 4:4), making freedom possible for us all. As we minister to our brothers and sisters involved in sexual sin, let us emulate the grace Christ showed to the woman caught in adultery. "Jesus said to her, 'Woman, where are they? Did no one condemn you?' She said, 'No one, Lord.' And Jesus said, 'I do not condemn you, either. Go. From now on sin no more'" (John 8:10–11).

Chapter 5

Lying and Stealing

You shall not steal, nor deal falsely, nor lie to one another.
—Leviticus 19:11

One of the more interesting parts of my job is talking to people about their lives. Given my chosen area of research—impulsive and aggressive behavior—it is safe to say that I have interviewed many fascinating people over the years. None have been more colorful than Gene.

I met Gene through his younger brother Ron, a local attorney. The contrast between these two men was remarkable. Ron was a successful lawyer and had a wonderful, loving family. He was active in his church and respected in his community. Gene, who was fifty years old at the time of our meeting, had recently been released from prison after serving two years of a four-year sentence for issuing worthless checks. As part of his early release, he had been court-ordered to have a psychological evaluation, which was what brought him to me.

As we talked, Gene began to describe his troubled past. He had been arrested several times, usually for running some type of con. His incarceration for writing bad checks was the second time he had been in prison. Many years earlier he had served time for a real-estate scam he had concocted that took advantage of the elderly. Two failed marriages had produced an adult son, whom he rarely saw, and a teenager daughter, who longed for a deeper relationship with him—the father she barely knew. Gene had struggled for many years with a cocaine addiction, though at the time of our meeting he said that habit was "under control." And while he said that he had been attending a support group for help, Gene acknowledged that gambling was a significant problem in his life.

Though he had gone to college for only two years, he described his occupation as a legal/political/criminal-justice consultant. This was perhaps the most interesting thing about Gene: despite a troubled past, which he realized I knew about, he presented himself as a successful businessman. He rationalized or explained away his past problems, placing the blame on others rather than on himself. In his mind, he was simply misunderstood. The usual social standards—and even the laws—that we all live by didn't necessarily apply to him. Gene saw himself as special, better than others. He showed little remorse for his past crimes and transgressions; manipulating or using others was simply a means to an end.

Looking back, I think the saddest aspect of my interaction with Gene was observing how a little brother, Ron, was desperately trying to save the older brother he sincerely loved yet hardly knew.

BIOLOGY AND CRIME

The idea that criminality might be influenced by biological factors is not new. Cesare Lombroso (1835–1909), a Jewish-Italian criminologist, is often considered the father of this line of scientific investigation.

Lombroso believed that criminality was inherited, that there were certain individuals who were simply "born criminal." To him these individuals were evolutionary throwbacks, savage, and animalistic. He believed they could be identified through a set of physical "defects" such as large jaws, sloping foreheads, shifty eyes, and hawklike noses. Lombroso spent much of his career trying to develop a scientific methodology to predict criminal behavior based on these physical "defects."

While Lombroso was considered a pioneer of scientific criminology, his theories were ultimately proved wrong and are considered pseudoscience today. Though physical characteristics are not useful in the prediction of an individual's involvement in criminal behavior, the idea, however, that inherited biological traits such as impulsiveness, risk taking, and fearlessness may predispose an individual to antisocial behavior is being actively investigated by behavioral scientists today.

PREVALENCE

An estimated 9.8 million people are held in prisons throughout the world. Unfortunately, this number is steadily growing, suggesting that men and women like Gene are more common than we may want to admit. The United States has the highest prison population rate in the world (756 per 100,000 of the national population), followed by Russia (629) and Rwanda (604). In the United States in 2008, over 14 million arrests were made, and 7.3 million individuals (3.2 percent of adults in the United States) were incarcerated or on probation or parole.[1] For a country struggling through a major economic crisis, the annual costs of crime and victimization are staggering.

Based on the most recent figures (2003), the United States spends more than $185 billion for police protection ($83.1 billion), corrections ($60.9 billion), and judicial and legal activities ($41.6 billion) annually. Judicial expenditures account for approximately 7.2 percent of all state and local expenditures.[2] The total annual economic loss to victims is $1.1 billion for violent crime and almost $15 billion for property crime. Overall, the total cost of criminal behavior in the United States exceeds $1 trillion annually. To put this number in context, that is $4,118 for every person in the population.[3]

THE SCIENCE OF CRIMINALITY

In chapter 3, I described how dysfunction of the prefrontal cortex (PFC) increases the likelihood that an individual will engage in impulsive and/or aggressive behavior. A person with such a neurological dysfunction would also be predisposed to commit violent crimes such as assault or murder. While the thought that biology might play a role in violent crime is relatively well accepted, the same cannot be said of property offenses like burglary and arson. Is it possible that an individual could inherit a biological profile that would increase the likelihood that he or she would violate the laws of society? To try to answer this question, I will focus on a psychiatric disorder that occurs in approximately 75 percent of all incarcerated inmates: antisocial personality disorder.[4]

Types of Dramatic-Erratic Personality Disorders

A personality disorder is a rigid, ingrained pattern of thoughts and behaviors that deviates significantly from the expectations of society. This maladaptive pattern is usually well established by late adolescence or early adulthood and is serious enough to cause distress or impaired functioning. People with a personality disorder are usually unaware that their thoughts and behaviors are inappropriate, so they tend not to seek help on their own.

The American Psychiatric Association's diagnostics manual, *Diagnostic and Statistical Manual of Mental Disorders* (DSM-IV-TR),[5] lists antisocial personality disorder as one of the dramatic-erratic (also called Cluster B) personality disorders. While each of these personality disorders carries a separate and distinct diagnosis, they all share a number of overlapping and related symptoms, including problems with emotional expression and difficulty forming stable, healthy relationships. In addition to antisocial, the other dramatic-erratic personality disorders are borderline, histrionic, and narcissistic.

Antisocial personality disorder (ASPD) is characterized by a pattern of behavior that involves the manipulation, exploitation, or violation of the rights of others. Individuals with ASPD are often deceitful, lack remorse for their actions, and show an unwillingness to conform to social norms and laws. Gene, whom I introduced at the beginning of this chapter, met the criteria for ASPD.

Borderline personality disorder (BPD) is characterized by a persistent pattern of emotional instability, volatile interpersonal relationships, unstable self-image, and self-destructive impulsive behaviors.[6] Histrionic personality disorder (HPD) is characterized by a pattern of excessive emotional expression and attention seeking. Individuals with HPD often behave dramatically in situations that do not justify this type of reaction. They have an excessive need for approval and are often inappropriately sexually seductive or provocative. Narcissistic personality disorder (NPD) is characterized by extreme feelings of self-importance, a great need for admiration, and a lack of empathy. Individuals with NPD often exploit others for their own gain and are overly sensitive to criticism, judgment, or defeat.

ASPD Diagnosis and Treatment

Approximately 1 percent of the population of the United States is thought to meet the diagnostic criteria for ASPD in a given year.[7] Significantly higher prevalence rates are associated with prison settings (about 75 percent) and substance abuse treatment settings (about 22 percent).[8] The disorder occurs more than twice as often in men than women.[9] While the course of the disorder is chronic (lifelong), it may become less evident or remit as the individual moves into middle age (approximately forty years old).

To be diagnosed with ASPD, an individual must be at least eighteen years old and have shown some symptoms of conduct disorder (a pattern of socially destructive behaviors during childhood that may include aggression toward people or animals, destruction of property, deceitfulness, theft, truancy, or running away) before the age of fifteen. He or she must also have shown "a pervasive pattern of disregard for and violation of the rights of others" since age fifteen, as indicated by three (or more) of the following:

1. Failure to conform to social norms with respect to lawful behaviors, as indicated by repeatedly performing acts that are grounds for arrest.
2. Deceitfulness, as indicated by repeated lying, use of aliases, or conning others for personal profit or pleasure.
3. Impulsivity or failure to plan ahead.
4. Irritability and aggressiveness, as indicated by repeated physical fights or assaults.
5. Reckless disregard for safety of self or others.
6. Consistent irresponsibility, as indicated by repeated failure to sustain consistent work behavior or honor financial obligations.
7. Lack of remorse, as indicated by being indifferent to or rationalizing having hurt, mistreated, or stolen from another.[10]

A number of other disorders and problems have been shown to co-occur with ASPD, including depression, drug/alcohol abuse, anxiety disorders, and pathological gambling. Individuals with this disorder have an increased risk of dying prematurely by violent means (i.e., suicide, homicide). Long periods of unemployment, interrupted education, separation/divorce, abusive and neglectful parenting, homelessness, and frequent incarcerations are common with this disorder.

Because individuals with ASPD rarely seek treatment on their own, the judicial system is likely the most common referral source. While psychotherapy is the treatment of choice, its effectiveness in personality disorders is limited. Medications may be used to help stabilize mood swings or other co-occurring psychiatric conditions. There is no clinical research, however, that supports the use of medication for the direct treatment of ASPD.

Brain Mechanisms

Individuals diagnosed with ASPD have consistently been shown to be chronically underaroused.[11] In fact, a low resting level of physiological arousal in boys at age fifteen has been shown to predict involvement in criminal behavior at age twenty-four.[12] Traditional measures of physiological arousal include heart rate, skin conductance, and electroencephalography (EEG). Low heart rate and skin conductance activity (a measure of the amount of sweat on the skin) and increased slowing in the EEG are all indicators of less-than-average physiological arousal.

You might think of physiological arousal as your brain's level of activation. Imagine a dimmer switch connected to a light bulb. When the switch is turned all the way up, the maximum amount of electricity is available to the bulb, and it therefore shines brightly. Now imagine that you turn the switch halfway down. The bulb is still illuminated, but it lacks the necessary power to light up the room fully. That's what an underaroused brain is like: the "power" necessary for effective processing is simply not available.

So how could low physiological arousal predispose an individual to antisocial or criminal behavior?

There are two main theories that attempt to explain this link. The first we might call the fearlessness theory. This theory suggests that low levels of physiological arousal at rest are reflective of low levels of anxiety and fear. Lack of fear would predispose an individual to antisocial and criminal behavior because such behavior requires a degree of fearlessness. In addition, a lack of anxiety and fear during childhood would significantly limit an individual's ability to learn from the negative consequences associated with wrong behavior. In other words, when there is no fear of punishment (because of physiological underarousal) for antisocial behavior, a person is unable to effectively learn what is considered socially appropriate.

The second theory that has been proposed to explain the link between low physiological arousal and antisocial behavior might be called the sensation-seeking theory. This theory suggests that low levels of arousal produce an unpleasant physiological condition. In other words, it doesn't feel good. Individuals in this unpleasant state are thought to seek out stimulation in an attempt to raise their level of arousal to a more optimal or normal level. Antisocial and criminal behaviors are then attempts to increase their level of physiological arousal. It isn't that they consciously choose only antisocial behaviors to increase their level of arousal; it is just that high-risk behaviors such as burglary or substance abuse are the only types of experiences that are positively stimulating and reinforcing to them.

The combined effect of these two theories is likely more important in explaining antisocial and criminal behavior than either one taken alone (see Figure 1). Underaroused individuals are less fearful (anxious) and actively seeking novel experiences and high levels of stimulation. It could be said that they are physiologically wired to be involved in dangerous and destructive behavior.

In addition to problems in physiological arousal, brain-imagining studies of violent criminals have consistently found reductions in the size[13] and functioning of the prefrontal cortex (PFC).[14] As I discussed in chapter 3, problems in PFC functioning can lead to impulsive and aggressive behavior (see Figure 6). Taken together, these results suggest that low resting levels of physiological arousal predispose an individual to involvement in nonviolent antisocial behavior (e.g., burglary, arson). In contrast, low arousal in combination with deficits in prefrontal cortex functioning appears to increase the likelihood that an individual will commit a violent offense (e.g., assault, murder).

Heritability

Much like the heritability of impulsive aggressive behavior, a large body of evidence from both twin studies and adoption studies suggests that there is a genetic predisposition for criminality.

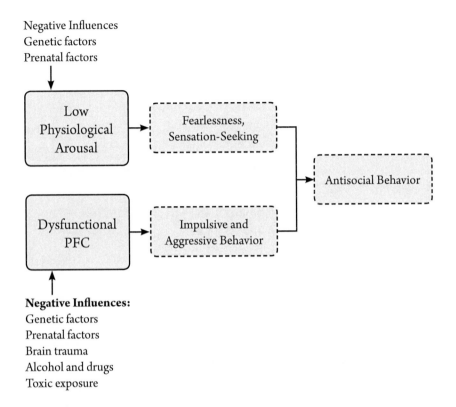

Negative Influences
Genetic factors
Prenatal factors

Low
Physiological
Arousal

Fearlessness,
Sensation-Seeking

Antisocial Behavior

Dysfunctional
PFC

Impulsive and
Aggressive Behavior

Negative Influences:
Genetic factors
Prenatal factors
Brain trauma
Alcohol and drugs
Toxic exposure

Figure 6. Overview of Biological Factors Influencing Antisocial Behavior

Two large reviews of the existing twin studies of criminality found that the concordance rate for monozygotic (identical) twins is 51 percent, while the concordance rate for dizygotic (fraternal) twins is 21 percent.[15] A 51 percent concordance rate in identical twins means that if one of the twins is a criminal, then there is a 51 percent chance that the other twin will also be a criminal. Higher concordance rates for identical twins, who share 100 percent of the same genes, compared to fraternal twins, who share only 50 percent, suggest that there is a heritable or genetic aspect to crime.

A second way that genetic influences on behavior are assessed is through the use of adoption studies (see chapter 3 for a description). An extensive review of the existing adoption studies looking at criminality found that virtually all showed a clear genetic basis for antisocial behavior.[16]

Together, twin and adoption studies show us that an individual's risk of being involved in criminality increases significantly with the presence of criminal behavior in his or her biological relatives.

Neurochemistry

Cortisol, also called glucocorticoid, is a stress hormone that is secreted by the adrenal glands (located on top of the kidneys) during times of stress and anxiety. When normal individuals are aroused or stressed, they show an increase in cortisol. Several studies looking at cortisol levels (using mainly saliva or blood samples) in criminal populations have found below-normal levels.[17] This result would be expected because antisocial individuals are relatively fearless (less intimidated or threatened by their environment) as a result of their low physiological arousal.

A second neurochemical important in criminality is serotonin, an inhibitory neurotransmitter found in the brain. Low serotonin functioning has been demonstrated in numerous studies of antisocial and criminal populations.[18] As I explained in chapter 3, the serotonin system has been shown to control the activity of areas in the prefrontal cortex. Less serotonin leads to reduced activity in the PFC, which results in a person having less ability to control his or her behavior. Problems in the serotonin system appear to be more related to violent criminal offenses than to criminality in general.

A Newfound Faith

Karen's troubles began even before she was born, as her addicted mother exposed her to intravenous drugs throughout the pregnancy. Her parents divorced when she was three. With no father in the home and an addict as a mother, Karen had little guidance and supervision as a child. It wasn't long before she fell in with the wrong crowd and became involved in delinquent behavior. She was a discipline problem in school, even as a young child, and was expelled or suspended numerous times. By the tender age of fourteen she already had a long history of fighting, drug use, stealing, and truancy and had been caught bringing a weapon to school. That year, for the first time, she was sent to live at the state home for girls.

Released a year later, Karen successfully completed the eighth grade (the highest grade she would complete). But then she ran away from home and was caught shoplifting, which led to a second stay at the state home for girls. When she was released upon turning eighteen, Karen had little to show from her childhood other than an extensive criminal history and a heavy addiction to drugs and alcohol.

Karen's adult life was much like her childhood and adolescence. Multiple arrests for drug possession and theft led to four extended periods of incarceration. In the periods between imprisonments, she was hospitalized multiple times for depression and suicidal thoughts. Once she tried to end her life by ingesting rat poison mixed into milk. Karen never married, but she moved from one physically abusive relationship to another. One time her boyfriend stabbed her in the forehead, but she refused to go to a hospital because she was wanted by the police.

When I met Karen, she was thirty-three years old. She had been released from prison three weeks earlier and was interested in getting into a drug and alcohol treatment program, which was why she was referred to me. My clinical assessment showed that she met the diagnostic criteria for substance dependence and antisocial personality disorder. Neuropsychological assessment of her cognitive function showed mild frontal-lobe dysfunction.

Karen told me that every other time she had gotten out of jail or prison she had started using drugs and stealing the next day, but that this time was different. During her last stay in prison, she had come to faith in Christ. Karen now wanted to change, and she believed her newfound faith in God was helping her to maintain her sobriety and to focus on turning her life around.

THE STUBBORN AND REBELLIOUS SON

The Old Testament contains a number of references to criminal behavior, including assault (Exodus 21:18), murder for hire (Deuteronomy

27:25), kidnapping (Exodus 21:16), extortion (Leviticus 6:2), theft (Deuteronomy 5:19), and slander (Leviticus 19:16). In the New Testament, we see that individuals who were guilty of criminal behavior became followers of Jesus (Mark 2:14–15; Luke 19:8–9) and part of the first-century church (1 Corinthians 6:7–11; Ephesians 4:28).

What about antisocial personality disorder? Can we find an account of such a biologically driven disorder in the Scriptures? I believe we can in the description of the "stubborn and rebellious son" found in Deuteronomy 21:18–21. The Talmud, an ancient record of Jewish laws and traditions, quotes the Jewish rabbis as stating that Ezekiel 18:10–13 also refers to the "stubborn and rebellious son." Let's look at these two passages together:

> If any man has a stubborn and rebellious son who will not obey his father or his mother, and when they chastise him, he will not even listen to them, then his father and mother shall seize him, and bring him out to the elders of his city at the gateway of his hometown. They shall say to the elders of his city, "This son of ours is stubborn and rebellious, he will not obey us, he is a glutton and a drunkard." Then all the men of his city shall stone him to death; so you shall remove the evil from your midst, and all Israel will hear of it and fear. (Deuteronomy 21:18–21)

> Then he may have a violent son who sheds blood and who does any of these things to a brother (though he himself did not do any of these things), that is, he even eats at the mountain shrines, and defiles his neighbor's wife, oppresses the poor and needy, commits robbery, does not restore a pledge, but lifts up his eyes to the idols and commits abomination, he lends money on interest and takes increase; will he live? He will not live! He has committed all these abominations, he will surely be put to death; his blood will be on his own head. (Ezekiel 18:10–13)

These passages have intrigued psychiatrists for years because they so closely mimic the criteria necessary for a diagnosis of antisocial personality disorder.[19] Sister Elizabeth Bellefontaine gives a vivid description of this troubled young man:

> His excessive eating and drinking ran counter to accepted social norms. . . . These particular vices suggest that he was a non-productive, non-contributing parasite in the community. Being undisciplined and unpredictable, he would be untrustworthy in time of crises such as war. At any time, his unrestrained behavior could have offended others and strained inter-family or inter-clan relationships, risking retaliation or feud against himself, his family and his community. Then there was the peril of the divine wrath which might fall upon all the people because of the presence of the evil-doer in their midst. Thus, the son's deviant behavior not only corrupted him but may have meant serious negative consequences for his neighbors.[20]

When one compares the biblical description of the "stubborn and rebellious son" with the diagnostic criteria for antisocial personality disorder, it is clear that this young man displays "a pervasive pattern of disregard for and violation of the rights of others" and meets all seven of the DSM-IV-TR criteria (only three are needed for a diagnosis of antisocial personality disorder; see criteria above). The presence of antisocial personality disorder in biblical times suggests that the disorder is not simply the result of modern cultural or societal influences, since ancient Israel and twenty-first century America are very different, but is further evidence of an underlying biological basis to the disorder.

The "stubborn and rebellious son" was also spiritually disordered. All other Old Testament references to being "stubborn and rebellious" are associated with Israel's unfaithfulness to God (Psalm 78:8; Jeremiah 5:23), and indeed at the core of the "stubborn and rebellious" son's sinful behavior is the fact that he had turned from the one true God to worship pagan idols (Ezekiel 18:11–12). For his antisocial and criminal behavior, the "stubborn and rebellious son" was sentenced to death by public stoning so that all Israel would know the terrible consequences of sin and, in response, turn to God.

SETTING THE CAPTIVES FREE

My friend Gary is a mild-mannered man in his midsixties. After twenty years of service in the military, he retired and opened a small clock-repair shop. He still tinkers with clocks, but his true passion is evangelism. Every Sunday afternoon you will find him in the same place, standing in a roomful of people and proclaiming the good news of salvation. What makes this Sunday gospel presentation unique is that it takes place behind the walls and gates of a state prison and that the people being ministered to are all inmates. More specifically, they are youthful offenders: children ten to seventeen years old who have been convicted of crimes and are incarcerated by the state. Gary has been going to this particular facility for eight years. He told me that the first time he walked through the gates of this prison he felt the presence of God come upon him like he never had before.

During his first visit to the adolescent facility, as he watched another man sharing the gospel with the children, Gary sensed God speaking these words to him: *You know how they feel.* From that day forward he saw his troubled childhood differently. "God prepared me for ministering to these children," he explains. "When they say to me, 'You don't know what it's like to be me,' I tell them my story."

The oldest of five children, Gary grew up in a very dysfunctional family. His father was an alcoholic, and he physically abused Gary and his siblings. Even though he was only seven years old at the time, Gary vividly remembers his parents' divorce proceedings in which they argued over who would have to take the children, since neither wanted them. More mistreatment and neglect would follow from a string of abusive stepparents. Gary describes his childhood as "hell on earth." To escape the madness of his home life, Gary would often catch a bus to the local Baptist church on Sundays. Sitting in church one Sunday morning when he was sixteen, enjoying the calm and peace for a few hours, he heard the gospel for the first time—and his life was changed forever.

Gary's involvement in prison ministry started at a young age. As an eighteen-year-old enlisted man in the air force stationed in Georgia, he would drive each week to a local civilian airfield for flight lessons (Gary dreamed of becoming a missionary pilot who would bring the gospel to the most remote parts of the world). Every day his drive would take him past a large state prison. He often wondered about the men inside, and one day he impulsively decided to pull into the prison and check it out. Segregation in the South during the early sixties extended even to prisoners, and Gary quickly found out that this prison was for black men, aged forty and over, who were sentenced for life. He was able to meet with the warden and ask him if anyone was visiting these men in order to share the gospel with them. The warden's answer was no, so Gary asked if he could start visiting the inmates to minister to them. The warden said he would only allow an ordained minister to visit the men, and Gary had no such credentials. However, the warden did agree that if Gary could get a minister to come with him, he would be allowed to visit also. So Gary went straight to the base chaplain and recruited him to start visiting the prison.

It was tough going at first; two white men in an all-black prison in the Deep South didn't draw a big crowd. Only a few inmates attended at first, and their motivation was simply to get out of their cells for an hour. Gary told me it took about six months before some of the men started to be interested in the gospel. "God began to soften their hearts," he said. It was a full year before anyone came to faith in Christ.

During a recent conversation with Gary, I asked him to tell me a story that would help others understand his passion about ministering at the youth prison. With tears in his eyes, he told me about the following occasion.

"I had spent time preparing a lesson that week—like I do every week—for my Sunday afternoon time at the prison. But as I began to teach, a young man raised his hand and asked me, 'What do I say to my mother?'

"I asked him what he meant, and he said, 'She is dying of cancer and will not live long enough to see me get out of here. She is coming to visit me next Thursday, and it will probably be the last time I ever see her. What do I say to her?'

"That's when you forget the lesson!" Gary said. "The rest of the hour we just ministered to that young man. I told him, 'The first thing you tell her is that you love her. You look her straight in the eyes and tell her how much you love her. Then you apologize. Tell her how sorry you are that the mistakes you made in the past have become a burden for her. After that, tell her that you want her to be in heaven with you for eternity.'"

Gary then described to the young man how he might share the gospel with his dying mother. A troubled child, discarded and forgotten by society, was set free by the power of Christ to become a minister of the living God. That's why Gary is so passionate about prison ministry!

MINISTERING TO THOSE IN PRISON

God has a heart for prisoners. Listen to Jesus' own words to his followers:

> But when the Son of Man comes in His glory, and all the angels with Him, then He will sit on His glorious throne. All the nations will be gathered before Him. . . . Then the King will say to those on His right, "Come, you who are blessed of My Father, inherit the kingdom prepared for you from the foundation of the world. For I was hungry, and you gave Me something to eat; I was thirsty, and you gave Me something to drink; I was a stranger, and you invited Me in; naked, and you clothed Me; I was sick, and you visited Me; *I was in prison, and you came to Me.*" Then the righteous will answer Him, "Lord, when did we see You hungry, and feed You, or thirsty, and give

You something to drink? And when did we see You a stranger, and invite You in, or naked, and clothe You? When did we see You sick, or *in prison, and come to You?*" The King will answer and say to them, "Truly I say to you, to the extent that you did it to one of these brothers of Mine, even the least of them, you did it to Me." (Matthew 25:31–40; emphasis added)

It is clear from these verses that God's people are called to minister to prisoners. And when we do, it is as if we are ministering to Christ himself. God's grace is available to everyone. Through the power of Christ, lives can be changed; past sins can be forgiven. So how might you get involved?

Not everyone is like Gary and will just drive down to the local jail or prison and start a ministry from scratch, though that is certainly an option. If that kind of evangelism isn't your style, make contact with an established ministry like Chuck Colson's Prison Fellowship. Through such a ministry you will have opportunities for everything from giving financial support to volunteering your time. Take, for example, Prison Fellowship's Angel Tree ministry, which reaches out to children who have a parent in prison. For the price of a Christmas gift, a child's life can be impacted by the love of Christ. You can find additional information about prison ministries at the end of this book.

I hope this chapter has convinced you that a subset of people are indeed born more impulsive and less fearful than others and that, because of this, they are more likely to become involved in antisocial and criminal behavior. This fact in no way minimizes an individual's responsibility for his or her actions, but it does help us better understand that sin is pervasive and has a hold on us both spiritually and physically. While receiving Christ by faith fully transforms us spiritually (2 Corinthians 5:17), it does not alter our physical bodies. Physically, we all still struggle with sin; and the journey toward sanctification lasts a lifetime.

The writer of Hebrews calls us to "remember the prisoners, as though in prison with them" (Hebrews 13:3). We who are in the body of Christ know all too well what it is to be in bondage. In our hopeless state, while we were still prisoners of sin, Christ came to set us free (Romans 5:6–8). He calls us, former captives, to do the same to share the good news of our release. Whether a person is sitting in his or her living room or in an eight-by-eight concrete cell, true freedom is available only through a relationship with Jesus Christ.

Chapter 6

Addiction

Let us behave properly as in the day,
not in carousing and drunkenness.
—Romans 13:13

To most people, Frank and Lisa looked like the all-American Christian couple. Good looking, charming, and self-assured, Frank was a successful executive recruiter. Lisa, a petite and attractive brunette, was a dedicated wife and mother and was actively involved in the women's ministry at their church. A survivor of a physically abusive first marriage, Lisa brought two daughters into her relationship with Frank, and together they had a young son. The family lived in a beautiful two-story home on a tree-lined street near a lake. The only thing that seemed out of place in this "perfect" family portrait was the tremendous sadness one could often see in Lisa's eyes.

Frank began drinking when he was fourteen. Adolescent experimentation quickly turned into an all-consuming addiction. Now forty-two, Frank was drinking a pint of Vodka and two or three beers every day—and had been for many years. His first marriage had lasted only a year because of his addiction. Frank would become verbally abusive when intoxicated, and Lisa was often the target of his outbursts.

Sitting in my office, Frank described to me how he was once again trying to stop drinking. In May he had gone cold turkey and been detoxed at a local substance abuse treatment facility. Released after twenty-eight days, he soon began drinking again. Every day was a struggle to stay sober, but when the external stresses of life and the internal biological cravings for a drink would become too much, he gave in. By August he had completely fallen off the wagon and was drinking daily. After one of his drunken outbursts that month, Lisa threw him out of the house. That incident motivated him to volunteer for a study testing the effectiveness of naltrexone, a drug thought to minimize the craving for alcohol. Lisa allowed Frank to return home in early November, but by Thanksgiving she had thrown him out again.

When I met Frank in early January of the following year, he was still in the naltrexone study, attending Alcoholics Anonymous every day, and seeing a Christian counselor once a week. He had consumed alcohol only one day in the preceding month, and Lisa had recently allowed him to come home again. As with many alcoholics, this cycle of trying to stop drinking, relapsing, hitting bottom, and trying to stop again had become a regular pattern for Frank. It wasn't that he didn't want to stop drinking; he just didn't think he was strong enough to do it.

Frank struggled for several more months that year before going to live at a Christian treatment facility in another state, where he finally found the help that he needed to stop drinking. Today Frank and Lisa are truly the happy couple they appear to be. While Frank has had a few slips, his periods of sobriety are now marked in years rather than days, and he is clearly on the path to recovery.

ADDICTION

Since the beginning of human history, people have experimented with mind-altering substances. Archaeologists have found the residue of a fermented beverage of fruit, honey, and rice that was being consumed in northern China over nine thousand years ago.[1] As early as 3400 BC, the Sumerians of lower Mesopotamia (modern Iraq) were cultivating the opium poppy, which they referred to as the "joy plant." There has always been a subset of people who, like Frank, are unable to control their use of these intoxicating substances and become addicted to them.

No one who experiments with drugs or alcohol believes that he or she will experience the destructive effects of addiction. That's because addiction does not happen overnight, but experimentation and recreational use slowly increase until addiction becomes an all-encompassing way of life.

PREVALENCE

The use of intoxicating substances is extremely common. Based on 2007 survey data (the last year for which figures are available) gathered by the Substance Abuse and Mental Health Services Administration (SAMHSA), an estimated 19.9 million Americans aged twelve and older (approximately 8 percent of the population of that age group) report being current illicit drug users (meaning they used an illicit drug in the month prior to the survey), while about 126.8 million (approximately 51 percent of the population aged twelve and older) report being current drinkers of alcohol. It is estimated that among individuals who reported using drugs and/or alcohol in the previous year, approximately 22.3 million (around 9 percent of the US population aged twelve and older) were addicted. Of these, 69 percent (15.5 million) abused or were addicted to alcohol, 17 percent (3.7 million) abused or were addicted to an illicit drug, and

14 percent (3.2 million) abused or were addicted to both alcohol and illicit drugs.[2]

Addiction occurs more commonly in men, with an average age of onset between eighteen and thirty years old.[3] It has been found that the younger a person starts drinking or using drugs, the more likely he or she is to become addicted as an adult. For example, adolescents who use alcohol before the age of fifteen are four to five times more likely to become addicted than those who wait until their twenty-first birthday to start drinking. Another shocking statistic is that adults who use illicit drugs are more than twice as likely to have a serious mental illness (e.g., depression) than adults who do not use illicit drugs.

The high prevalence of addiction has resulted in staggering human and economic costs. Approximately one in four deaths each year is attributable to alcohol and substance abuse. More than 75 percent of domestic violence victims report that their assailants had been drinking or using illicit drugs at the time of their assault. It is estimated that 55 percent of all fatal automobile accidents are alcohol related. Since 1995, drug offenders have accounted for more than one-third of the growth in the state prison population and more than 80 percent of the increase in the number of federal inmates. The total economic burden of addiction on the US economy is estimated at over $400 billion annually.[4]

THE SCIENCE OF ADDICTION

Benjamin Rush, a founding father of the United States and a signer of the Declaration of Independence, is credited with first describing alcoholism as a "disease" in 1784. Prior to his writings on addiction, drunkenness was viewed as a moral defect and solely a matter of choice. Rush, a physician, believed that the alcoholic lost control of his behavior or had what he called "an illness of the will." He identified the properties of alcohol, rather than the individual's choice, as the causal agent. He also proposed that alcoholics could be treated by weaning them off their addiction using less potent substances (similar to the way that methadone is used for heroin addiction today) and that total abstinence was the only effective cure.[5]

Substance Use Disorders

The diagnostics manual for psychiatry and psychology (DSM-IV-TR) divides the substance use disorders into two categories that are reflective of the progression from drug or alcohol misuse to addiction.

Substance abuse is characterized by continued substance use despite frequent undesirable consequences related to that use. These consequences may include legal difficulties, loss of a job, health issues, neglect of a child, and/or marital problems. For diagnosis, this maladaptive pattern of use must have occurred repeatedly over a twelve-month period.

Substance dependence is characterized by a repeated pattern of substance abuse that can result in tolerance, withdrawal, and compulsive drug-taking behaviors. Dependence is what most people are referring to when they use the term *addiction*. Tolerance is present when the individual has to use progressively more of the substance over time to achieve a particular high. This tolerance is caused by compensatory responses in the body (e.g., liver enzymes) that oppose the effects of the drug and attempt to return the person to the state he or she was in before using the substance. Withdrawal is a set of unpleasant physical symptoms that are opposite of the effects of the drug. For example, if using the drug causes a decrease in heart rate, a potential withdrawal symptom might be an increase in heart rate. Withdrawal symptoms, like tolerance, are a result of the body's compensatory responses and appear when use of the drug is abruptly discontinued. If a person shows evidence of tolerance and withdrawal, he or she is said to have physiological dependence. Compulsive drug-taking behaviors include uncontrolled use of the drug, craving the drug, excessive amounts of time devoted to obtaining the drug, unsuccessful attempts to cut down or control substance use, and giving up important and pleasurable activities in order to obtain the drug. For a diagnosis of substance dependence, three or more symptoms must occur in the same twelve-month period.

The DSM-IV-TR lists ten classes of substances for which the diagnoses of substance abuse and dependence can be given: alcohol; amphetamines; cannabis (marijuana); cocaine; hallucinogens (e.g., LSD); inhalants (e.g., paint thinner); nicotine; opioids (e.g., heroin); phencyclidine (PCP); and sedative, hypnotic, and anxiolytic (antianxiety) substances (e.g., Valium, barbiturates, sleeping pills). A person is diagnosed with **polysubstance dependence** when he or she meets the criteria for substance dependence described above and has been repeatedly using at least three groups of substances over a twelve-month period.

People with drug and alcohol problems are often secretive about their substance use or blind to the fact that they even have a problem. Getting them to a point where a diagnosis of substance abuse or dependence can be made is difficult. But a proper diagnosis is important because it helps justify getting the person into a treatment program.

Brain Mechanisms

Over a lifetime, many people use substances that have the potential for dependence, but most people do not become dependent. What is it that causes recreational substance use in some people to become uncontrolled, compulsive drug-taking in others? The answer may have to do with how our brains respond to pleasure and rewards.

Have you ever wondered why you enjoy certain activities and aren't particularly interested in others? Things you enjoy are rewarding to you. In other words, they bring you pleasure, a sense of well-being, and reduced stress. All thoughts and behaviors have some biological component, and reward and pleasure are no exception. God has created within our brain a system that brings about a pleasurable experience when it is activated (see Figure 7A). Because we enjoy pleasurable experiences, we are more likely to repeat actions that activate our reward system. Many things can activate that system, from food to sex to alcohol and illicit drugs. For instance, food has been shown to increase activity in the reward system by 45 percent, whereas amphetamine and cocaine increase the activity by 500 percent.[6]

Commenting on this result, my graduate school pharmacology professor once said, "Cocaine takes your brain to a place it was never supposed to go, a place you will always try to get back to."

Imagine a person with a dysfunction in his or her reward system that causes the system to be underactivated. Things are not as rewarding to that individual as they are to the normal person. In neuroscience we call this condition reward deficiency syndrome.[7] Reward deficiency syndrome can result from an inherited genetic abnormality or from environmental factors such as trauma or stress. Research has shown that individuals with reward deficiency syndrome begin to seek out experiences that will increase activity in their reward system (see Figure 7B). If they experiment with alcohol or illicit drugs, initially they find the pleasurable experience they were seeking. But after a period of time, which will vary across individuals and

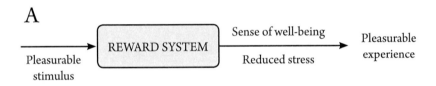

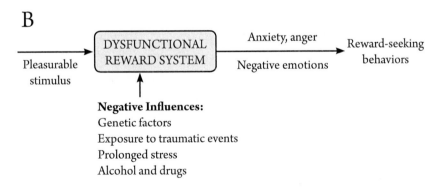

Figure 7. Overview of the Brain's Reward System

substances, a vicious cycle develops in which the consumption of alcohol and/or illicit drugs is no longer a choice or a pleasure but a necessity. The person becomes physically dependent on the substance and must take the drug to keep from experiencing painful and sometimes life-threatening withdrawal symptoms. While the positive, pleasurable state produced by the drug may have motivated initial use, continued use results in another motivation: relieving the negative, painful consequences of not using the drug.

Neurochemistry

While brain chemistry clearly plays a part, the underlying biological causes of the substance use disorders are much broader than any one neurotransmitter system. The reward system I have described above involves a number of brain structures, including the hypothalamus, amygdala, ventral tegmental area, substantia nigra, and nucleus accumbens. The nucleus accumbens, a structure deep within the middle of the brain, is considered by neuroscientists to be the brain's central reward center. The cells in this brain structure are activated by the neurotransmitter dopamine (DA). When DA is released in the nucleus accumbens, the results are increased feelings of well-being and reduced stress. Substances such as alcohol, cocaine, heroin, PCP, marijuana, and nicotine all cause DA to be released in the nucleus accumbens, and thus they are potentially addictive. In addition, the neurotransmitters serotonin and GABA (gamma-aminobutyric acid) also appear to play a role in the brain's reward system. Substance abuse and dependence involve a complex interaction between the physiological effects of drugs on the brain's reward system and the learning of compulsive patterns of drug-seeking behaviors, both of which have a biological basis.

Heritability

Research suggests that a genetic predisposition for addiction, much like the other behaviors I have discussed thus far, can be inherited from one's parents and grandparents. Several studies have found that the child of an addicted parent is about four times more likely than the general population (where the risk is one in twelve) to develop substance abuse or dependence themselves. This holds true even if the child of the addicted parent is adopted early and subsequently raised by adoptive parents who do not use alcohol or drugs.

As might be expected, a significant amount of genetic addiction research has focused on genes that are associated with the brain's dopamine system. Alcoholism researcher Ken Blum and his colleagues have shown that a defect in the gene that codes for the dopamine D2 receptor is associated with the presence of substance use disorders. Their research found that an individual with such a genetic defect has a 74 percent chance of developing reward deficiency syndrome.[8] It is important to remember that, unlike diseases such as hemophilia, sickle-cell anemia, and cystic fibrosis, which are caused by a defect in a single gene, behaviors like addiction are genetically complex and are likely to result from defects in many different genes.

Treatment

On any given day, millions of Americans receive treatment for problems related to the use of alcohol or illicit drugs. Data from the federal government showed that in 2007 an estimated 3.9 million people ages twelve and older reported receiving treatment for a substance use problem. Most were treated for an alcohol use problem (2.5 million), while 936,000 received treatment for marijuana, 809,000 for cocaine, 558,000 for pain relievers, 311,000 for stimulants, 335,000 for heroin, and 303,000 for hallucinogens.[9]

Treating substance use disorders is a long and difficult process, and relapses are common. It has been found that 40–70 percent of alcohol-dependent patients relapse within a year following treatment.[10] Ninety percent of treated alcoholics will experience at least one relapse within four years following treatment.[11] While addicts initially chose to use the substance they are now dependent upon, recovery is much more complicated than simply telling them to stop using the drug.

Detoxification. Before any treatment can begin, it is necessary for substance-dependent individuals to be detoxified. This means that all the substances they are addicted to are removed from their bodies. Since withdrawal can be severe and even life threatening, detoxification should always be done under the supervision of a medical doctor. By using a variety of medications, a physician can minimize the severity of withdrawal symptoms and gradually move a person through the detoxification process. Medications commonly used during detoxification include benzodiazepines, anticonvulsants, and antidepressants.

Psychotherapy. A wide variety of psychotherapeutic strategies have been developed for treating drug and alcohol dependence. Behavioral and cognitive approaches are two common psychotherapeutic techniques that are used. They are based on the assumption that addictions are learned behaviors. In the behavioral approach, the patient is taught how to handle stress and manage situations without alcohol. In cognitive therapy, an attempt is made to alter self-defeating thoughts (e.g., *I cannot tolerate anxiety*) and irrational beliefs (e.g., *I am helpless*) that drive a person to use drugs and alcohol. Psychotherapy may be done in inpatient or outpatient settings.

Relapse Prevention. Once an individual completes detox and inpatient treatment, the focus shifts to helping him or her avoid relapsing into drug and alcohol use. Relapse prevention may include a combination of medication, continued psychotherapy, and twelve-step programs. People recovering from substance dependence often show significant mood and anxiety problems. These problems may have preceded their substance dependence or have been caused by it. Left untreated, these problems can play a role in a person returning to substance abuse. For this reason, a variety of medications, such as antidepressants, antianxiety agents, and mood stabilizers, may be prescribed to reduce the symptoms.

Continued psychotherapy is necessary to help the patient identify stressful situations and objects in the environment that can trigger a relapse. Individuals who seek treatment are also referred to some type of twelve-step program. Twelve-step groups are composed entirely of recovering addicts, and involvement in the group is free. The first twelve-step program was Alcoholics Anonymous (AA), upon which all other programs have been based. The basic foundations of all twelve-step programs are the biblical concepts of submission, forgiveness, and accountability. The basic message reinforced by the group is that it is impossible for a person to stop being an addict as long as that person clings to the idea that he or she can ever again take a drink or use drugs. Recovering addicts are taught to significantly change the way they live in order to avoid a relapse.

Pharmacotherapy. Several medications have been developed to help the recovering individual avoid using again. These medications take two differing approaches to relapse prevention. First, disulfiram (Antabuse) is an alcohol-sensitizing medication. When combined with alcohol, it increases the level of acetaldehyde in the blood, leading to nausea, vomiting, headache, flushing, and other unpleasant effects. While this medication discourages alcohol use, it does not eliminate the desire or craving for alcohol. Second, calcium acetylhomotaurinate (Acamprosate) and naltrexone (ReVia) are anticraving medications. People using these medications don't get sick when they drink, but they often get less pleasure out of drinking and are less likely to want to drink again. Calcium acetylhomotaurinate appears to reduce cravings by affecting the GABA neurotransmitter system. Naltrexone interferes with dopamine, the neurotransmitter that produces pleasurable effects in the brain's reward system, thus blocking the high normally produced by alcohol. Naltrexone is also somewhat effective in treating relapse in opiate (e.g., heroin) dependence.

Daddy's Little Girl

Joanna was born in Germany, where her father was stationed as a member of the US military. While appearing happy on the outside, the family hid a dark secret and was in constant conflict. Joanna's father was an alcoholic and physically abused both her and her mother. After the birth of her brother, when she was five, Joanna adopted the role of mother/ protector and worked hard to make the home environment safe and happy for him. Trying to dull the pain from years of abuse, she began drinking and smoking marijuana at fifteen. "I wanted freedom," she told me. "I was unhappy with my parents trying to control me."

While Joanna would experiment with different drugs (marijuana, crack cocaine, prescription painkillers) through the years, alcohol was always her main addiction, as was the case with her father. Despite her heavy drinking, however, she was able to graduate from high school and complete three years of college. After twenty-five years of heavy drinking, the longest period of sobriety she could remember was thirty months. She has attended seven different alcohol treatment programs but relapsed soon after completing each.

Though never married, Joanna has been involved in a number of unhealthy and abusive relationships with men. Because of her addiction, she has been unable to hold a job for more than a few months at a time. "If I'm unhappy, I want to drink; and because I drink, I'm always unhappy." When I met Joanna, she had just completed her third week in a local faith-based inpatient drug treatment program with which I work.

Now thirty-five, Joanna has no relationship with her father and hasn't had for some time. As I listened to her story, I was struck by the amazing parallels between the life of a daughter left empty by the lack of a father's love and the life of a father who never appreciated the blessing he had been given. She likely began drinking both because of a genetic predisposition passed down to her from her father and because of the severe abuse that he inflicted on her. As an adult, Joanna continued to try to heal her pain by using alcohol and by moving from one abuser to another—recreating the father-daughter relationship that had so damaged her as a child. In 1997, her father was convicted of intoxication manslaughter and sentenced to prison for deaths he caused while driving drunk. Joanna herself has two convictions for driving while intoxicated. The legacy of this family, passed from generation to generation, is alcoholism and abuse. Joanna received it from her father, much like he—as she reported—had received it from his alcoholic father (Joanna's grandfather).

DRUNKENNESS IN THE FIRST-CENTURY CHURCH

It is clear from the scientific literature that biology does influence the initial use of drugs and alcohol in some individuals, and that biology, after prolonged use, perpetuates the problem through physical dependence. The Scriptures are also clear when it comes to this problem: "drunkenness" is a sin (Romans 13:13; 1 Corinthians 6:9–10; Galatians 5:19–21). The Bible does not prohibit or condemn the use of alcohol. In fact, Ecclesiastes 9:7 encourages readers to "drink your wine with a cheerful heart." Psalm 104:14–15 teaches that God gives "wine which makes man's heart glad." Jesus turned water into wine at the wedding feast at Cana (John 2:1–11). And Paul tells Timothy, "No longer drink water exclusively, but use a little wine for the sake of your stomach and your frequent ailments" (1 Timothy 5:23). What is sinful and prohibited is overindulgence that leads to a state of intoxication and addiction (Proverbs 23:29–35; Ephesians 5:18; 1 Timothy 3:8).

Addiction is not just a modern-day problem among believers, but was a significant issue even in the early Christian church. Paul calls the Roman church to behave properly and not to be involved in drunkenness (Romans 13:13). In Romans 14:21, he suggests that the moderate use of wine by some was causing others in the church to stumble. Some in the Corinthian church were using the Lord's Supper as a time to get drunk (1 Corinthians 11:21). In his letter to the Ephesians, Paul admonishes believers not to allow themselves to be controlled by wine but to submit to the control of the Holy Spirit (Ephesians 5:18). The Thessalonians were reminded that drunkenness is of the darkness and that, as "sons of light," they should be alert and sober (1 Thessalonians 5:4–8). Paul encourages Titus to teach the older women of Crete that it is not proper to be "enslaved to much wine" (Titus 2:3).

In the early church, excessive drinking disqualified a man from serving as an elder or deacon, an indication that some men in the fellowships were struggling with this problem (1 Timothy 3:3, 8; Titus 1:7). It is safe to say that struggles with alcohol abuse and dependence were widespread in the early church. Paul alludes to the subject in all his letters, with the exception of 2 Thessalonians and his letters to Philippi (Philippians) and Colossae (Colossians and Philemon), while Peter calls for the believers in the churches of Asia Minor to make a clean break from their pagan pasts, which included drunkenness and drinking parties (1 Peter 4:3). The good news, however, is that life transformation came to the addicted in the early church (1 Corinthians 6:9–11), just as it certainly comes today.

CONTROLLED BY CRYSTAL METH

Tim and Rachel grew up in Christian families. Both of their fathers served as deacons in the local church where they met. They were considered good kids, with great potential. But a poor decision resulted in Rachel becoming pregnant at the age of fifteen. Tim's parents didn't handle the situation well; they forbade Tim to see Rachel or his daughter, and ultimately they left their longtime church home out of shame. By the time they were nineteen, Tim and Rachel had begun dating again. They decided to get married, despite the protests of Tim's parents. Tim admits, "At nineteen, I wasn't ready to be married and have a three-year-old child. We were just immature kids ourselves."

Married life was difficult, and Tim and Rachel fought constantly. They began attending a new church and progressively became more and more involved, eventually leading worship during the Sunday morning services. Tim described his relationship with God at that time as more corporate than personal. The use of pornography was also becoming a problem for him. When they were twenty-one, Tim and Rachel had their second child, a son. Finances had always been a concern for the couple, so Tim was happy when Rachel's father found him a job in road construction. Tim, the youngest man on the crew, described the other men as a "rough crowd." Young, impressionable, and wanting to fit in, he jumped at the chance to go on a weekend deep-sea fishing trip with his coworkers. It was on that trip that Tim was first offered crystal meth (methamphetamine).

Crystal meth is a powerful stimulant. It is a member of the amphetamine family of drugs. Crystal meth comes in either icelike crystal chunks or a coarse powder, and is either smoked, snorted, or injected. Tim had never used any drugs before that trip, and he thought he would just do it once to fit in and then never do it again. "It felt really good. All the stresses of life, all the worries and problems, just disappeared." At work the following week, Tim was offered some crystal meth to use over the weekend. He gladly accepted. Soon he was using every Friday and Saturday, all the while keeping his increasing drug use from Rachel.

As Tim's weekend use increased, it became harder and harder to go to sleep (one of the effects of methamphetamine is insomnia), so he found himself drinking half a bottle of NyQuil at night just to get some rest. Exhausted, Tim discovered that it was more and more difficult to get up and go to work come Monday morning. He started buying a little extra crystal meth each week to use on Monday mornings, just to get him up and going. Friday and Saturday nights turned to three or four days a week, which quickly progressed to everyday use. "It owned me," Tim said. "After eight months of using every day, I was disgusted by my addiction. I tried to stop using several times, but I would feel terrible and become so irritable that it would result in more fighting with Rachel, which would convince me that quitting now was a bad idea—and I would start using again."

Tim had been able to keep his addiction a secret from Rachel, but foreclosure letters and overdue bills made her begin to wonder where their money was going. In an attempt to find out, Rachel looked through their credit card bills and came across a charge to a strip club. When Tim came home that evening, Rachel angrily confronted him about the charge. That was when Tim told her about his addiction to meth. "I decided that if my marriage was going to end, I was going to get it all out." Rachel was shocked by the news. They sought counsel from a friend, who was also a pastor, and set in motion a plan for Tim to stop using and to be held accountable through random drug tests that Rachel would administer. They continued to lead worship through all of this, choosing not to tell their pastor or anyone at their church about the situation. They were fearful and ashamed.

Tim was able to stay clean for a while, but he slowly began using again. When he started failing his drug tests, Rachel gave him an ultimatum: "Go to rehab—or I'm taking the kids and leaving." Tim pleaded with her, swearing that he would change. But he didn't. He told me, "I just got better at fooling her." About this same time, Tim began playing guitar in a country music band. Rachel didn't like it that Tim was playing in bars every weekend, given his problems with lust and drugs. She was right to be concerned, because about then Tim began having an adulterous relationship with a former high school girlfriend.

To hide his drug use and affair, Tim would sometimes be gone for days at a time. Rachel knew something was going on, so when she had the opportunity, she looked through Tim's cell phone. Finding text messages from the other woman, she immediately ordered Tim out of the house. Rachel called their pastor and told him the whole story. His only response was to tell her that, biblically, she was released from the marriage. That wasn't what she was looking for; she wanted to hear something more.

Tim said, "At that moment I realized that I had hit rock bottom. I was about to lose everything. Despite the way I was acting and the things I was doing, I loved my wife and kids. I broke off the affair and stopped using meth that day (although I would relapse several times)." Rachel sought out another pastor, and Tim agreed to go for marital counseling. This pastor offered something different from the first: hope. He said, "While it will be difficult and may take some time, God can heal your marriage." They received individual and marital pastoral counseling for several months.

That was four years ago. Today, Rachel and Tim's marriage is stronger than ever. They are very open about their struggles and about the miracle that God has done in their lives. When I asked Tim what the most important thing that he learned from his experience was, he immediately replied, "The Father-heart of God. God was there all the time, wanting me to come home and give my problems to him; but I kept running away. You are never too far gone for God. After God delivered me from my addiction, I remember asking him, *How can you love me?* And he responded, *How can I not?!*"

MINISTERING TO THOSE
STRUGGLING WITH ADDICTION

Christian counselor and author Ed Welch describes those who struggle with addiction as slaves or prisoners. Of the addictive experience he wrote, "It may be incredibly unwise, but we care more about the way it makes us feel at the moment, and we wind up enslaved to the substance and behaviors that once brought us pleasure and release." He says that the addict is "both in control and out of control," and he characterizes the addictive experience as both rebelliousness and bondage.[12] For true and complete recovery, all three aspects of the addict's being (body, mind, and spirit) will need treatment and ministry.

Because spiritual bondage is at the heart of the substance use disorders, when we minister to those struggling with addiction it is imperative that we focus on the freedom believers have in Christ. The Scriptures are clear that even Christians can become enslaved or mastered by sinful desires (1 Corinthians 6:12; 2 Peter 2:19). We must remind our addicted brothers and sisters that Christ came to set us free from bondage to sin. We can use Isaiah 61:1 to illustrate this truth: "The Spirit of the Lord GOD is upon me, because the LORD has anointed me to bring good news to the afflicted; He has sent me to bind up the brokenhearted, to proclaim *liberty to captives* and *freedom to prisoners*" (emphasis added).

Christ's redemptive work is complete, and in him we are truly free from sin. Many believers, however, choose to live in bondage to their own fleshly desires rather than in freedom. Paul admonishes us in Galatians 5:1: "It was for freedom that Christ set us free; therefore keep standing firm and do not be subject again to a yoke of slavery." We must help those struggling with addiction to see that they can choose either to live free in Christ or to be a slave to their fleshly desires. Christ's redemptive work has transformed them into a new creation if they have received him by faith (1 Corinthians

6:9–11), but they still must choose whether to be controlled by wine or controlled by the Spirit (Ephesians 5:18).

In addition, we must understand that a few Bible verses and a quick prayer are not going to break the death grip of addiction. Relapse is common and should be expected. When we minister to those struggling with substance use, we must be prepared to walk alongside them for the long term—through the good times and the bad.

Chapter 7

Homosexuality

You shall not lie with a male as one lies with a female;
it is an abomination.
—Leviticus 18:22

Caitlyn first noticed that she was attracted to girls at age twelve. It bothered her; she knew that she was somehow different. In an attempt to suppress her same-sex attraction, she became very promiscuous with boys. "I knew it was wrong. I was trying to overcompensate with guys, but it made me feel even guiltier." After years of trying to suppress her thoughts and feelings, she eventually came out to her best friend; and shortly thereafter she told her parents. Neither handled it well. In fact, that was the last time she spoke to her best friend, who told her that she would need to change if they were going to continue to be friends. Now twenty-one, Caitlyn lives openly as a lesbian with her girlfriend of one year.

Caitlyn grew up in a Christian family. She was homeschooled through high school and then attended a small Christian college. Since coming out a year ago, she has returned to the conservative church she grew up in only a few times. "They have basically shunned me. To them, I have committed an unforgivable sin, so I just don't go to church anymore. I still believe in God; I pray; I'm just not in church."

Caitlyn sees her parents about once a week. They won't let her bring her partner to their home, and to prevent them from interfering with her life and relationship, she has not told them where she lives or given them her phone number. On the other hand, her partner's parents, who are not believers, have accepted the couple with open arms. Caitlyn wishes she could have the same type of relationship with her parents. "I'm not asking them to accept my homosexuality. I know that it is wrong; I know what the Bible says. I just want them to love me like they used to."

I asked Caitlyn what she would like to say to Christians in regard to homosexuality. With great emotion, she responded, "Why is this sin different than all the others? The church accepts people back that commit every other sin—adultery, divorce. Why not homosexuality? Jesus hung out with sinners, but I've been shunned by the church. Once you admit that you're gay, you're an outcast in the eyes of the church. If this is the 'Christian' way to reach homosexuals, then it is the wrong approach. I'm not asking that you accept my behavior. But at least care about me as person; be my friend. Isn't that what Jesus would do?"

A HOUSE DIVIDED

Homosexuality may be the most divisive issue of our time and has been called "the greatest crisis in the church today."[1] Like issues of race a generation ago, the topic of homosexuality is dividing communities, churches, and families. So it is with great caution and abundant grace that I step into the fray in this chapter. In the abstract, anyone can state an opinion by arranging a set of important-sounding words on a page, but we have to remember that we are talking about real people with feelings and emotions, people who have been created in the very image of God (Genesis 1:26). We also have to realize that this is not an "us versus them" conflict; personal struggles with homosexuality are a reality for many Christians in the church today. Never was this more apparent to me than just this week when Mark, a worship pastor friend of mine, called, seeking my advice.

Mark shared with me that his longtime friend Andrew, a leader on their church worship team who has a wife and two children, told him that he had been struggling to suppress homosexual thoughts and feelings for many years. Andrew confessed that five years earlier he had a brief homosexual affair with another married man. And now he had decided to embrace his "homosexual identity" and divorce his wife. Struggling alone and in silence for so many years had left him exhausted and no closer to the freedom for which he longed. He said that he simply couldn't do it anymore. At great cost, Andrew was now going to embrace a way of life he had always considered sinful in the eyes of God. The cost would be his marriage, his family, and perhaps his faith.

PREVALENCE

In my local newspaper, a recent editorial that was supportive of homosexuality made the claim that "homosexuality . . . occurs in as much as 10 percent of the population."[2] This 10 percent figure that is often reported for the prevalence of homosexuality can be attributed to the human sexuality research of Alfred Kinsey in the 1940s and 1950s. Most people are surprised to find out that Kinsey never actually reported that he found 10 percent of the population to be homosexual. What he did report was that, from his sample, "10 percent of white males were more or less exclusively homosexual for at least three years between the ages of 16 and 55."[3] Much of Kinsey's work has been discredited because he used a highly biased sample for his studies. Behavioral scientists now consider the 10 percent figure to be an extreme overestimation.[4] In fact, Paul Gebhard, the second director of the Kinsey Institute, lowered the estimate from 10 percent to 4 percent, following a reanalysis of Kinsey's original data, and tried to remove some of that bias.[5]

So how prevalent is homosexuality today?

To answer this question, I reviewed the existing scientific literature on human sexual behavior. This included data from the United States, Canada, the United Kingdom, Denmark, France, Norway, and Australia. I found that definitions of what constitutes homosexuality and homosexual behavior have varied widely, as have prevalence estimates. It seems to me that two numbers are important to know: the prevalence of homosexual (same-sex) experiences and the prevalence of those who identify themselves as exclusively homosexual. To determine the prevalence of homosexual experiences, I combined data from fourteen studies (conducted between 1988 and 2003) that asked participants if they had ever had a same-sex sexual experience, either since adulthood or anytime during the last ten years. This resulted in an estimate of 5 percent for men and 7 percent for women, meaning that about 6 percent of the general population reports having had a homosexual experience as an adult. But what percentage of these individuals would be classified as exclusively homosexual?

For that estimate, I combined data from twelve studies (conducted between 1977 and 2003) in which the participants either identified themselves as exclusively homosexual (versus heterosexual or bisexual) or reported having sex only with same-sex partners for at least the last five years. This resulted in an estimate of 2 percent for men and 1 percent for women.[6] In the United States, that would mean there are slightly less than 4 million individuals (1.5 percent of the population fifteen and older) who are exclusively homosexual.

THE SCIENCE OF SEXUAL ORIENTATION

Sexual orientation is the degree of romantic or sexual attraction an individual experiences toward either men or women. Individuals who show a consistent preference for sexual relations with members of the opposite sex are said to have a *heterosexual* orientation, while those who show a preference for sexual relations with members of the same sex are said to have a *homosexual* orientation. A small number of individuals are relatively ambivalent about their sexual partner's gender and are therefore considered *bisexual* (sexually attracted to both men and women). The biological study of sexual orientation, specifically homosexuality, is a very hot topic in neuroscience, and presently the majority of scientific evidence suggests that a problem in the sexual differentiation of the brain early in development results in a homosexual orientation.

Sexual Differentiation

Every cell of your body contains twenty-three pairs of chromosomes. The DNA that makes up those twenty-three pairs of chromosomes contains all the genetic information needed to make another you. The information contained in twenty-two of those chromosome pairs determined your physical development apart from your sex. The last pair consists of two sex chromosomes, and it is this set of genetic information that determines if you are a male or a female. There are two types of sex chromosomes: X chromosomes and Y chromosomes. Females have two X chromosomes (XX), and males have both an X and a Y chromosome (XY). An individual's genetic sex (XX or XY) is determined at the time of conception.

All the genetic information needed to develop the body and behavior of either a male or a female is contained in the X chromosome and the twenty-two nonsex chromosomes found in the cells of every individual. Through the sixth week of development, male and female fetuses are physically identical. Each contains tissue that has the potential of developing into male or female sex organs. It is the Y chromosome, which is only present in the male, that causes this undifferentiated tissue to develop into testes. When the Y chromosome is not present, as in the XX female, this tissue develops into ovaries. The function of the testes and ovaries is to produce sex hormones, and it is exposure to these hormones both before and after birth that produces the physical and behavioral differences seen between men and women.

Sexual Inversion

In utero, the male fetus is bathed in androgens produced by the newly formed testes. Exposure to androgens during prenatal development has a masculinizing effect on the fetus and promotes the development of anatomical and behavioral characteristics typical of males. The testes also release androgens that have a defeminizing effect by preventing the female reproductive system from developing. The female fetus, in contrast, develops anatomical and behavioral characteristics typical of females because it is not exposed to androgens in utero. So you might say that the default biological program is to develop a female unless androgens are present.

In the case of a male with a homosexual orientation, it is thought that a problem in early androgen exposure results in an incomplete masculinization of the brain, allowing the development of feminine neuroanatomical and behavioral characteristics. In the homosexual female, it is thought that the reverse occurs: abnormal exposure to high levels of androgens in utero causes masculinization and defeminization, resulting in neuroanatomical and behavioral characteristics typical of males.

This reversal of brains and behavior has been referred to as a sexual inversion, and there are three indirect behavioral sources of evidence that support this theory.

First, since this theory is based on a dysfunction in early sex hormone exposure, which is a process that predominately occurs in the developing male fetus (remember the default is to make a female), homosexuality should be more common among males than females. Indeed, as I mentioned earlier in regard to prevalence, that is exactly what occurs: homosexual orientation occurs more often in men than in women.

Second, since an individual is born with this sexual inversion, then behaviors typical of the opposite sex (such as boys preferring to play with dolls)—called childhood gender nonconformity—should be more prevalent in young children who later develop a homosexual orientation. Research shows that childhood gender nonconformity is strongly related to adult homosexual orientation. Gay men typically report having been feminine boys, while lesbian women were masculine girls.

Finally, according to the sexual inversion theory, adult homosexuals should show a higher frequency of behaviors and interests typical of the opposite sex. Studies focusing on masculinity/femininity in adult homosexuals have found that gay men are typically more feminine and lesbian women more masculine than their heterosexual peers.[7]

Behavioral differences are interesting, but if this theory is correct, we should also be able to identify structural brain differences between homosexuals and heterosexuals. Specifically, we should find that areas of the brain known to be involved in sexual behavior appear more feminine in organization in male homosexuals and more masculine in organization in lesbian women.

Brain Mechanisms

The area of the brain that has been most studied in regard to homosexuality is the hypothalamus. This small structure located near the bottom of the brain controls an amazing variety of behaviors, ranging from heart rate to eating to sexual activity. In chapter 4, I described how the hypothalamus is involved in our sex drive and long-term attachment system. From research with both humans and animals, we know that several areas (each called a nucleus) within the anterior hypothalamus are *sexually dimorphic*, meaning that these areas develop differently in the two sexes.

The first reported neuroanatomical difference between homosexuals and heterosexuals was found in the suprachiasmatic nucleus (SCN). The SCN is an area in the anterior hypothalamus that is involved in biological rhythms and sexual behavior. Normally the SCN is larger and more elongated in women than in men. The SCN has been shown to be larger and more elongated in homosexual men than in heterosexual men, having the shape and size characteristically found in women.[8] Another sexually dimorphic area of the anterior hypothalamus, the third interstitial nucleus of the anterior hypothalamus (INAH3), has also been found to differ in homosexual males. The INAH3 is usually smaller in women compared to men. Several studies have found that the INAH3 is smaller in homosexual men than in heterosexual men, suggesting a more femalelike anterior hypothalamus.[9]

A very similar result was recently found in a study of transsexuals—individuals who, despite being genetically and physically male or female, believe that they belong to the opposite sex. This conviction is so strong that these individuals often choose to have sex-change surgery. This condition is different from homosexuality, but these two groups have similar sexual orientations. Male-to-female transsexuals live as women and are sexually attracted to men, while female-to-male transsexuals live as men and are sexually attracted to women. A recent study found that the INAH3 of male-to-female transsexuals was similar to heterosexual females and that the INAH3 of female-to-male transsexuals was within the normal range for heterosexual males.[10]

A final piece of evidence that links sexual inversion in the anterior hypothalamus to homosexuality comes from research with sheep. It is estimated that as many as 10 percent of rams show a sexual partner preference for other males. This is the only known animal species (other than man) that shows exclusive homosexual behavior independent of human intervention. Similar to the human studies I have just described, a sexually dimorphic nucleus (oSDN) has also been found in the anterior hypothalamus of the sheep. The oSDN is normally larger in rams (males) than ewes (females). However, the oSDN in male-oriented (homosexual) rams has been shown to be smaller than in female-oriented (heterosexual) rams and similar in size to ewes.[11]

Taken together, these studies suggest that the anterior hypothalamus is involved in sexual orientation. Sexual preference for male or female sexual partners appears to be dependent on the level of masculinization or feminization of this neural structure during prenatal development. So what exactly is causing this sexual inversion in the brains of individuals with a homosexual orientation? To answer that question, we must look more closely at the hormonal environment that a fetus is exposed to during development.

Neurochemistry

Since most of the work in the neurobiology of homosexuality has been done with males, let's first look at the hormonal environment of the male fetus. As previously mentioned, the testes of the developing male fetus produce androgens. The most important of these, for our discussion, is testosterone. As testosterone is released by the testes to masculinize the fetus, some of it is changed by enzymes in the fetus's brain into other important hormones. One of those enzymes is a substance called aromatase. The function of aromatase is to convert testosterone into estradiol. Estradiol then masculinizes the areas of the brain high in estrogen receptors. The anterior hypothalamus is one such area, and aromatase activity is very high there (see Figure 8A). It has been suggested that a lack of aromatase activity in the fetal brain results in the neuroanatomical and behavioral differences seen in the male homosexual (see Figure 8B).

Support for this theory comes from studies that have looked at sexual behavior in animals. For example, if male rats are treated prenatally and postnatally with a substance that inhibits the activity of aromatase, they show bisexual behavior as adults. In addition, an examination of their brains reveals that their suprachiasmatic nucleus (SCN), located in the anterior hypothalamus, is larger than in untreated male rats.[12] This is consistent with the larger SCN found in human male homosexuals, as I described above.

Additional evidence for reduced aromatase activity in the anterior hypothalamus of male homosexuals comes from the male-oriented rams I mentioned earlier. When the brains of these "homosexual" rams are examined, specifically the oSDN in the anterior hypothalamus, they are found to show reduced aromatase activity compared to female-oriented (heterosexual) rams.[13] Again, this supports the idea that homosexual orientation in men may be the result of an undermasculinized (more femi-nized) anterior hypothalamus.

In females, the picture is not quite so clear. For the sexual inversion theory of homosexuality to hold up, the brains of lesbians—or at least parts of them—should be masculinized. The most likely cause of this would be increased prenatal androgen exposure, but how that occurs is still, as yet, unknown. There are two potential sources of androgens to which the developing female fetus might be exposed: circulating maternal testosterone and androgens secreted by the fetus's own adrenal glands. Several studies have shown that females prenatally exposed to high levels

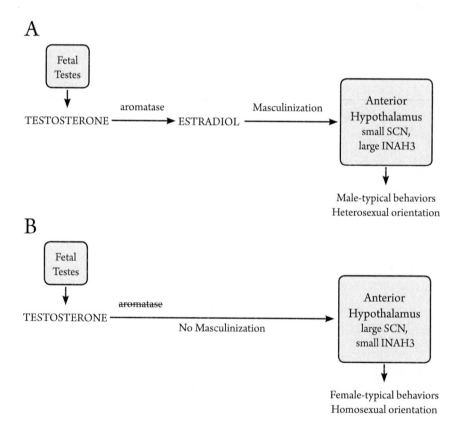

Figure 8. Overview of Male Homosexual Orientation

of maternal testosterone show more male-typical behaviors and interests as both children and adults.[14]

The best evidence for a link between female homosexual orientation and brain masculinization (caused by prenatal androgen exposure) comes from research with individuals who suffer from a genetic disorder called congenital adrenal hyperplasia (CAH). In CAH, a genetically mediated enzyme deficiency causes the adrenal glands of the fetus to produce excessive amounts of androgens during development. Worldwide, newborn screening suggests that CAH occurs in one in 14,500 live births. The disorder occurs in both sexes, but its effects on the female fetus are of the most interest. Research finds that girls with CAH are behaviorally masculinized, meaning they show more male-typical behaviors and interests.[15] As adults, women with CAH report higher rates of bisexuality and homosexuality than women without the disorder.[16]

Taken together, these studies are supportive of the sexual inversion theory and demonstrate that females exposed prenatally to high levels of androgens are masculinized and report differences in sexual orientation.

Heritability

Just as we have seen that rage, lust, criminality, and addictions are all influenced by heredity, so is homosexuality. Family studies find that homosexual men and women have more homosexual brothers and sisters than do their heterosexual peers. Twin studies (see chapter 3 for explanation) have shown a greater concordance for homosexuality in monozygotic (identical) twins compared to dizygotic (fraternal) twins.[17]

Genetics researcher Dean Hamer has suggested that a set of genes on the X chromosome may influence male sexual orientation. His studies have shown that this X-linked genetic marker is shared by approximately 64 percent of gay brothers.[18] As I have said previously, behaviors like homosexuality are complex phenomena that result from an interaction between biological predispositions and environmental triggers. Several environmental factors have also been linked to homosexuality, including family dysfunction, an older father, late birth order, the number of older brothers, and maternal stress during pregnancy.

CHANGING SEXUAL ORIENTATION

In 1973, the American Psychiatric Association voted to remove homosexuality from the *Diagnostic and Statistical Manual of Mental Disorders* (DSM). Soon after, the American Psychological Association endorsed the psychiatrists' decision. Thus, homosexuality was no longer considered a mental disorder, which further widened the chasm between the mental health and faith communities. Conservative Christians often tell me that this development has caused them to distrust all things related to psychiatry and psychology.

The American Psychiatric Association did preserve, in the third edition of the DSM, a category of dysfunction related to distress over one's homosexual orientation, called ego-dystonic (i.e., unwanted, distressing) homosexuality. In the present edition of the diagnostics manual (DSM-IV-TR), this problem is now listed under "sexual disorders not otherwise specified" and is defined as persistent and marked distress about sexual orientation.[19] So while psychiatry and psychology do not recognize homosexuality as a disorder in and of itself, they do recognize that having a homosexual orientation is distressing for some individuals because of societal pressure and/or religious values.

Many individuals distressed by their homosexual orientation seek assistance from therapists or ministries in the hope that they might be able to change. Therapy with the goal of changing homosexual orientation, often referred to as "reparative therapy," is practiced by a small number of psychologists and psychoanalysts. Reparative therapists believe that homosexuality is a developmental disorder that results from poor attachment to the same-sex parent during childhood. It is thought that if this disrupted same-sex attachment can be developed in the therapeutic relationship, then the individual will be able to overcome his or her homosexuality. Many therapists who practice reparative therapy belong to the National

Association for Research and Therapy of Homosexuality (NARTH), an organization that promotes the idea that a homosexual orientation can be changed.

A second set of individuals who offer assistance in changing one's homosexual orientation is often referred to as "ex-gay ministries," the most well-known of which is Exodus International. These ministries tend to view the causes of homosexuality similarly to reparative therapists, but they focus on the transforming power of faith, rather than a particular therapeutic approach, to change sexual orientation.

Finally, Sexual Addicts Anonymous (SAA), a twelve-step program based on the principles and traditions of Alcoholics Anonymous, views homosexuality as a compulsive sexual behavior and believes that being in fellowship with individuals struggling with similar issues brings freedom through dependence on a higher power, shared experiences, and accountability. Collectively, these three approaches that share a common focus on changing homosexual orientation are often referred to as "conversion therapies," a term that I will use throughout the remainder of this chapter.

Before we look at studies that have assessed change of orientation, it is important that we have a better conceptualization of sexual orientation. Sexual orientation is often thought of as a set of separate categories (e.g., a person is either heterosexual or homosexual). These categories are thought to be distinct and not to overlap. Research has shown, however, that this idea of distinct categories is simply not correct; sexual orientation actually lies along a continuum.[20] A majority of people fall at one end of the continuum and are exclusively heterosexual. As we move along the continuum, we encounter individuals who could be described as predominantly heterosexual. At the midpoint of the continuum, we find individuals who would describe themselves as bisexual, meaning they are equally attracted to men and women. As we move a little further, we encounter those best described as predominantly homosexual, although they still have some heterosexual tendencies. Finally, at the opposite end of the continuum, we find individuals who are exclusively homosexual in orientation.

Viewed this way, a change in sexual orientation would be best thought of as movement along the continuum toward greater heterosexuality, as opposed to jumping from one category to another. With this in mind, I reviewed recent studies that have tried to assess the potential for changing one's homosexual orientation.

While a complete change from an exclusively homosexual orientation to an exclusively heterosexual orientation only occurs in a small number of individuals, published studies are consistent in showing that a majority of those who are distressed by their homosexual orientation and receive some type of conversion therapy do have a shift toward increased heterosexuality.[21] Individuals who consider conversion therapy to have been successful in changing their sexual orientation appear to fall into three groups:

- those still struggling to control homosexual fantasies and behavior
- those not struggling to control homosexual fantasies and behavior
- those who have had a complete heterosexual shift

Additionally, research suggests that women show greater change than men and that religiously based interventions appear to be more effective than secular therapy.

HOMOSEXUALITY AND THE BIBLE

The simple sense of the Scriptures is that homosexual behavior is sinful (Genesis 19; Leviticus 18:22, 20:13; Romans 1:26–27; 1 Corinthians 6:9–10; 1 Timothy 1:9–10; 2 Peter 2:7; Jude 7) and that the divinely instituted norm for human sexuality is faithfulness in marriage between a man and a woman (Genesis 1:27, 2:24; Matthew 19:4–6) and chastity in singleness (1 Corinthians 6:15–20, 7:8–9). However, as we were reminded by Caitlyn at the beginning of this chapter, we yearn to know how Jesus himself, the friend of sinners (Luke 7:34), interacted with and responded to those involved in homosexuality. Jesus' own words in Matthew 19:1–12 give us some idea.

Challenged by the Pharisees on the topic of divorce, Jesus affirmed the divine intent of God that men and women who married would stay together for a lifetime (vv. 4–6). Divorce for any reason other than sexual immorality, Jesus taught, is simply not an option (vv. 8–9). Jesus' own disciples were concerned by this radical teaching, retorting, "If the relationship of the man with his wife is like this, it is better not to marry" (v. 10). In Jesus' day, parents arranged marriages, and betrothed couples were not allowed to spend time alone together until after the wedding. The prospect of marrying with no way out of a potentially bad match seemed worse to the disciples than not marrying at all.

Responding to their objection, Jesus replied that choosing not to marry is a serious matter and that only those who are called by God to such a life should attempt it (v. 11). He then described three types of eunuchs: those "who were born that way from their mother's womb," those "who were made eunuchs by men," and those "who made themselves eunuchs for the sake of the kingdom of heaven" (v. 12).

Jesus' graphic statement would have shocked those listening. Traditionally, those "who were made eunuchs by men" were men who were castrated, often against their will, for service in the royal palace or in wealthy households. Because their condition lowered their social status and made it impossible for them to have a family of their own, they were considered more trustworthy and less likely to try to usurp the position of the king or the head of the household. They were often used to serve and guard the women of the household (for an example, see Esther 2:14). To the Jews of the first century, eunuchs were seen as less than men. They were likely considered unclean and outside the covenant and were forbidden to enter the temple (Leviticus 21:17–20; Deuteronomy 23:1).

Jesus then referred to those "who made themselves eunuchs for the sake of the kingdom of heaven." This reference applied to men (and women) who had chosen unmarried celibacy so that they might dedicate themselves to a life of service to God. Paul discussed this same topic in 1 Corinthians 7:32–35.

But who were those Jesus described as eunuchs "who were born that way from their mother's womb"? Biblical scholar Robert Gagnon says, "The phrase 'eunuchs who were born thus from their mother's womb' is probably an inclusive group consisting of any man who lacks sexual interest in women. This group would include both men who have genital abnormalities that result in impotence and men whose genitals are still capable of begetting children. It would also include both asexual persons and persons who, in time, develop exclusive same-sex attractions."[22] So Jesus apparently made reference to a group that historically was known to include homosexual men.[23]

In no way am I saying that Jesus was endorsing homosexual behavior. He was simply saying that a special measure of God's grace is required for those called to a life of unmarried celibacy, and then he made reference to a group that likely included homosexuals as one such example. Jesus' reference to this ostracized class of men, equating them in a sense to those who have chosen a life of service to God, is yet another example of God's abundant grace. Considered unclean and barred from intimacy with God in the temple, a eunuch (regardless of the type) was an outcast. Yet listen to God calling to his lost children through the prophet Isaiah: "To the eunuchs who keep My Sabbaths, and choose what pleases Me, and hold fast My covenant, to them I will give in My house and within My walls a memorial, and a name better than that of sons and daughters; I will give them an everlasting name which will not be cut off" (Isaiah 56:4–5). So God seeks a relationship with the outcasts—intimacy and honor for those the world considers unclean and too damaged for the family of the King. We see this vividly played out in the story of Philip and the Ethiopian eunuch in the Book of Acts (8:25–40).

Philip, one of the original seven called out for service to the church (Acts 6:5), was directed by an angel of the Lord to the desert region south of Jerusalem. There he found a eunuch, treasurer to the queen of

Ethiopia, sitting in his chariot, reading Isaiah. One interpretation of the text suggests that the man had traveled a great distance to worship at the temple in Jerusalem, only to be turned away because he was both a Gentile and a eunuch. Feeling worthless and humiliated as he returned to his homeland, he struggled to understand the words of the prophet that had driven him to seek out the God of the Israelites. His frustration was clear when Philip asked him if he understood what he was reading. "Well, how could I, unless someone guides me?" he replied. Philip, empowered by the Holy Spirit, then began to teach the man about Jesus—and he was forever transformed.

Philip didn't first question the Ethiopian about what type of eunuch he was or how he came to be one. He simply did what the Spirit had empowered him to do: share the words of life. That day the call of God in Isaiah 56 was realized in the life of the Ethiopian eunuch, as a new name was written in the "book of life" (Philippians 4:3; Revelation 20:12).

OUT IN THE LIGHT

James is a full-time missionary to Muslims. He and his wife and three children have spent many years sharing the gospel in some of the most dangerous places in the world. I was grateful for the opportunity to support James as he shared with me about his struggles with homosexual thoughts and feelings.

James grew up in a Christian family. He had one sibling, an older sister. He said that he was a very sensitive child. In fact, he was often labeled as such by adults, which caused him to be quite insecure. "Because of the 'sensitive child' label, by the time I was in elementary school I really thought that there was something wrong with me, that I was different. I felt inadequate at sports, and prior to the fourth grade I never really had any close male friends—only female friends."

From a young age, James remembers being involved in sex play (i.e., "I'll show you mine if you show me yours") with girls. The first of these experiences that he remembers, however, was with a twelve-year-old male cousin when he was three or four. "I would say that I was involved in that kind of behavior more than the average child. I now believe that it opened a sexual side of me that the enemy was able to use."

By the time he entered junior high, James felt himself drawn more to males than to females. "Women were known to me—my mother, sister, friends. Men were a mystery. I had very limited male influences as a young child; the only male that had ever really been in my life was my father." At age thirteen, James was exposed to pornography. "A friend of mine had a magazine that he showed me. I remember that I liked looking at the women, but I also wanted to see men." Soon after that, James began masturbating regularly, and many times his sexual fantasies would turn to men.

It was when James was a sophomore in high school that he first began to think he might be gay. "I remember that I used to spend the night at a friend's house, and we would both sleep in his bed. It was totally innocent, but I felt drawn to him. I wanted to be close to him while we slept. I would roll over as close as I could during the night. I also remember wanting to see men in sexual situations in movies, television, and magazines. I began masturbating to that type of material."

In an attempt to fit in and be accepted, James started drinking and partying when he was a junior. His parents sent him to a Christian youth camp the summer before his senior year. There he was convicted to begin seeking a daily, living relationship with God. He stopped drinking, but his fantasizing and masturbating continued.

After graduating from high school, James enrolled in a Christian college. "I was terrified to take a shower in the dorm's community bathroom. I was afraid that I might get an erection if I saw other naked men, so I got up early before everyone else to shower. I knew my thoughts and feelings were wrong, but I felt like I didn't have anyone I could talk to."

Seeking a closer relationship with God, James joined a campus Bible study during his freshman year. "I remember that one week the topic for the Bible study was going to be homosexuality. I decided that I wasn't going to go that week. For some reason, I thought that people would realize I was gay. As the day of the study got closer, I felt more and more convicted by God that I should go. I'm glad I did. It was there that I first heard there was hope for someone like me who was struggling with homosexual thoughts and feelings, that my problem wasn't uncommon, that I wasn't alone. After the meeting, I just wept. I felt God's presence and peace like never before."

As James began to grow in his intimacy with God, he felt more open to share about his struggles, starting with his Bible study leader. "His response was great. He didn't pull back; he didn't reject me. He was supportive and prayed with me. I was so happy that someone else knew. It had finally been brought into the light." After that, James's homosexual thoughts and feelings started to occur less and less often. "As I would be open about my struggle, it became less difficult. I found that sharing about my struggle brought freedom."

On occasion, James still has homosexual thoughts and feelings. He has established a strong accountability system with other Christian men, and he also shares with his wife when he is struggling. "It is only by the grace of God that I am where I am today. If the right circumstances had presented themselves early in my life, I think I may have gone into the gay lifestyle. Today I find that the power of my thoughts and feelings are broken as soon as I confess that I am struggling. To me, living in freedom and victory doesn't mean that I never have a homosexual thought or feeling; it means that when the temptation comes, I don't give in."

MINISTERING TO THOSE
STRUGGLING WITH HOMOSEXUALITY

We treat it like no other sin. We want those involved in homosexuality to clean themselves up before they come to the church . . . before they come to God. The sad truth is that when we communicate that, we pervert the gospel (see Romans 5:8). Christ is in the business of transformation; and we need to trust that just as he saves, he sanctifies. We do that for other sins, such as divorce and addiction. A generation ago, divorce was taboo. Today we live in a culture that allows divorce for any and all reasons. Jesus taught that if a person divorces and marries another, he or she commits adultery and is involved in an ongoing sinful relationship (Matthew 19:8–9). Divorce is a rebellion against the very will of God (Malachi 2:10–16), yet the church's response to those who are divorced and seeking Christ has been an outstretched hand of redemption and grace—as it should be!

The sin of addiction is a constant cycle of struggle, relapse, repentance, and renewed struggle; yet the church supports those men and women as they slowly make the journey toward freedom. That is the process of sanctification, as we, empowered by the indwelling Spirit, struggle against our sinful flesh. If that same process doesn't work for the homosexual, then there is no place for any of us in the family of God. Albert Mohler, president of Southern Baptist Seminary, says it this way: "Our ministry to homosexuals is not as the sinless ministering to sinners, but as fellow sinners who bear testimony to the reality of salvation through faith in Jesus Christ."[24]

Life transformation for individuals struggling with homosexuality happened in the first-century church (1 Corinthians 6:9–11), and it can still happen today. As a church, we must be more accepting of gays and lesbians. They should be received into our fellowships with no questions or strings attached, as others are.[25] When they are moved by the Spirit to seek a more intimate relationship with Christ, in love we need to encourage change, to the extent it is possible, and chastity outside of a marriage between a man and a woman.

The fact is that men and women struggling with homosexuality are already in the church. Some are celibate and struggling to suppress their homosexual desires and feelings alone and in silence, while others have a spouse of the opposite sex and are struggling to suppress their homosexual thoughts and feelings—again alone and in silence. I see this as the great spiritual challenge of our generation. Either we will rise to the challenge and extend grace, like Philip, allowing Christ to draw these men and women to himself, or we will continue to stand as a barrier between Christ and his lost sons and daughters.

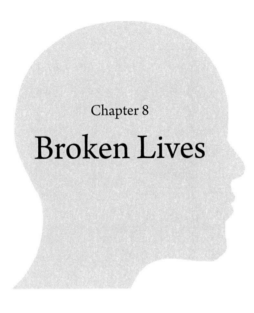

Chapter 8

Broken Lives

The LORD is near to the brokenhearted
and saves those who are crushed in spirit.
—Psalm 34:18

T he effects of sin are far-reaching. The suggestion that individuals hurt only themselves through their poor choices
is simply not reality (Exodus 20:5, 34:7). Hidden sin is
destructive; it undermines relationships and debilitates families. Once
exposed, sin produces a violent shock wave that damages everyone in its
path (see Luke 8:17). In many instances, the resulting physical, psychological, and spiritual wounds are so deep that they will be felt for a lifetime.
This chapter focuses on innocent women and children whose lives have
been broken by selfish, sinful choices. As I listened to their stories, I was

reminded of how desperately we need a Savior; and I pray that as you read them, you will be also.

LIVING WITH A STRANGER

The extreme mood swings were what Rachel first noticed.[1] "Tim would blow up at anything. He would seem fine one minute, but the next minute he would fly into a rage—yelling, screaming, hitting the wall. One time while we were driving, he threatened to bash my head into the windshield of the car. I was scared of him. I also noticed that he wasn't sleeping. He would stay up long after I went to bed. I thought he was staying up to look at pornography on the computer (a problem he had long struggled with). I never imagined that he was addicted to crystal meth."

Because crystal meth (methamphetamine) is a stimulant, those who abuse it often stay up for days at a time. "When Tim did sleep, it would usually be all day. He was late for work so often that they demoted him. I didn't know who he was anymore. It felt like I was living with a total stranger." Tim had never used drugs before he was offered crystal meth by a coworker on a weekend fishing trip. His recreational drug use quickly turned into a daily addiction. He also began drinking heavily. Despite his daily drug use, Tim would clean himself up every Sunday morning, and he and Rachel would lead worship at their church. Rachel naively continued to believe his excuses for his strange behavior and long absences from the family.

While finances had always been a struggle for the young couple, Rachel started to notice that their bills were not being paid; and then they received a foreclosure notice in the mail. "I wanted to know where our money was going. I started to think that Tim might be having an affair, or maybe he was drinking away all the money, so I started checking into our finances. First I found out that Tim had canceled our car insurance, which he explained as a mistake on the company's part. Then I started looking through our bank and credit card statements. I noticed that several hundred dollars were being withdrawn from our account every week and that this had been occurring for many months. I also found a large charge on one of our credit cards for a strip club. At that point, I still thought Tim must be having an affair, so I confronted him with what I had found and said that I wanted a divorce. That's when he told me about the crystal meth."

Tim explained everything to Rachel and begged her to stay. He swore that he would stop using. After doing some research on crystal meth and seeking counsel from a pastor friend, Rachel decided to stay. Tim agreed to take random drug tests, which Rachel would administer, and to meet regularly with some men who would hold him accountable. He was able to stay clean for a few weeks, but then he started using again. When his drug tests started coming up positive, Rachel demanded he go to rehab. But Tim just got better at hiding his addiction, and nothing changed.

As Tim's addiction progressed, he became even more verbally abusive at home. His ongoing problems with lust and his appetite for pornography were becoming more and more apparent. "When we were out, I would see him looking at other women. It hurt me. I still wanted my marriage to work, but not like this. I was starting to feel hopeless. I just couldn't continue to live like this anymore." During this time, Tim began having an affair with a woman he had dated in high school. To hide the affair and his continued drug use, he would be gone for days at a time.

Like many Christians, Rachel had always sought God during the difficult times of life but didn't have much of a relationship with him at other times. "Even though we were brought up in the church, Tim and I were Sunday-morning Christians. Our faith didn't mean much to us during the week." But as her marriage spiraled out of control, Rachel began to seek daily comfort from God. "In the past, I would go to God as I had need but then quit doing so when everything got better. This time was different—I was consistent. Tim's problems and my great need drove me toward intimacy with God."

As Rachel's spiritual intimacy increased, the intimacy in her marriage ended. "Tim started saying that he didn't love me anymore and that I wasn't a good wife. He rejected me daily. He would say that I didn't cook enough or that I didn't do his laundry right. So I started working harder at trying to be a better wife. I cooked more and went out of my way to please him, thinking that I was the problem. After a while, I just couldn't take it anymore and decided to get out of the marriage. I wasn't going to live like that any longer. I told Tim that we were moving in different directions; we had different morals, and I wasn't willing to compromise anymore. I remember praying a desperate prayer that God would restore my marriage. I prayed that God would break Tim so that he would seek his face. I had such a sense of peace after I prayed. It was about a week later that I found the text messages."

Looking through Tim's phone, Rachel found evidence of his affair. "When I found the text messages, I immediately thought about my prayer. The peace I had felt was gone. I feared that God was going to bring me down with Tim." Rachel confronted Tim about the affair and told him to get out.

Rachel called their pastor and told him what had happened. "All he did was tell me that I was released from the marriage, that I could get a divorce. He didn't even offer to pray with me. After I hung up the phone, I stood there and thought, *This is the end*. Tim begged me to stay. He said he would end the affair. He also told me that he was not using crystal meth, which I later found out was a lie." Rachel and Tim met with a local pastor, who offered very different counsel from their own pastor. "He spoke life and gave me hope. He told us that God could restore our marriage."

Tim recognized that he was about to lose everything, so he ended the affair and stopped using meth. That was four years ago. "It took years to work through everything, to be able to forgive Tim, and to let go of the anger. We are still working on some things. There were things in me that God needed to fix also. I saw myself as inadequate; I struggled with fear and a poor self-image. Our marriage today is better than I ever could have imagined. This was a terrible experience to go through; but if I knew that what we have now would be the result, I would go through it again. I received everything I prayed for, and I have witnessed God's faithfulness."

A SHAKEN FAITH

Like all little girls, Susan had dreamed of what her life would be like when she grew up. Those dreams often included the picture-perfect family: a strong, handsome husband who would love her forever and the healthy, beautiful children they would raise together. When Susan met Kevin in college, she believed those dreams were beginning to come true. Kevin was part of a college military-training program that was preparing him for service after graduation in the elite Navy SEALs. He was everything she had dreamed of: strong, handsome, and athletic.

Though raised in a strong Christian home, Susan was living the "normal" college life of too many parties and too much drinking when she met Kevin, who was living the same way. Susan described their dating relationship as "up and down." "Kevin was very hot and cold. Some days his affection was all-consuming. He couldn't get enough of me. He couldn't see me enough, talk to me enough, or be with me enough. During those times, he was also overly jealous. Other times he would ignore me and say, 'I don't know if I really love you.'"

Concerned about their relationship, Susan's parents cautioned her about marrying Kevin. "They had seen how he treated me, and they also questioned his Christian commitment." Nevertheless, after dating for two years, they got married. Susan became pregnant, and shortly before they both graduated, she gave birth to their daughter.

After graduation they moved to California so that Kevin could begin training for his service in the navy. "The first year after college was great. I had the husband that every woman wanted, and together we had the perfect family." After one year in California, the family moved to Virginia, where Kevin began his service. "He went from being home every day to being gone over two hundred days out of the year. He also started to be hot and cold, much like he had been when we were dating in college. Sometimes when he was home or called, he would smother me with love and attention, while other times he would be distant and cold. He never missed our daughter when he was away. One time, after being away for several months, he even told me that he hadn't missed us. He was drinking heavily and would regularly visit strip clubs with the other men in his unit when he was gone."

During this difficult time in their marriage, Susan became pregnant and gave birth to their second child, a son. As with their first child, Kevin didn't really want the baby and was absent and distant as a father. "I was so depressed, especially after the birth of our son. Kevin would call and say that he didn't love me anymore and that he didn't want to be married. I felt worthless and started blaming myself for our problems. I began having recurring nightmares that Kevin would abandon us; I feared that I would be unemployed and unable to care for my children. I was also starting to have thoughts about hurting myself, so I called my parents for help." Susan's father drove to Virginia and moved her and the children back home.

Within the first month of Susan's living with her parents, Kevin began calling. "He said he wanted me back. He wanted to fly me to Spain to be with him. When I asked him why he had said such hurtful things before, he just said, 'I don't know.'" Susan's visit to Spain went well, and when she returned to the States, she and the children quickly moved back to Virginia.

Susan told me that during this hard time she started crying out to God to restore her marriage. "I had moved far from my faith. Since getting married, I had tried several times to get involved with a local church, but Kevin was never supportive. I decided that I was going to give my all to God. I started praying regularly and attending a Bible study. I also (wrongly) blamed myself for our marital problems, and I dedicated myself to being a better wife."

After a short time in Virginia, the whole family moved to California so that Kevin could attend the navy's language school. "Everything changed for the better. Kevin was always home while he was going to school. He became the perfect family man. He showed more attention to me and the kids. He was drinking less, and we were attending church as a family. I started thanking God; I really believed that my prayers had been answered. God was restoring my family. It was the happiest time of my whole life."

After a year of language school, Kevin left for a six-month deployment. "I had to choose whether to stay in California during Kevin's deployment or move back in with my parents. I wisely chose to move back to my parents' house. It was Christmastime when Kevin came back, and he was like a different person. He was angry, depressed, and drinking heavily. He made it clear that he didn't want to be with our family. After three days, he said he needed some time alone, so he left to go skiing. He had been away from us for six months—and after three days he left. I now know he went to meet a girl, but at the time I didn't know what was going on."

Kevin moved back to California, while Susan and the children chose to stay with her parents. "On the phone everything would seem great. He would say that he loved me and that he missed me. He would visit us about once every six weeks. But when he visited, he showed no emotion. He was like two different people." Susan started getting counseling to help with her depression. She also continued to fast and pray for her marriage. "I remember begging God, in desperation, to release me from my marriage. I knew that I couldn't live like this forever."

Susan received a call from an old college friend who lived in New York during this time. "She said that she had heard Kevin and I were getting a divorce, and she just wanted to check on me. I told her I didn't know what she was talking about. She then told me about Kevin's girlfriend. I immediately called Kevin, and he of course denied that there was another woman. I knew he was lying, so I searched through our old cell phone bills, found a suspicious number, and called her. She said that Kevin had not told her that he was married. Though she did know about the kids, Kevin had lied and told her that he had a great relationship with them and was a dedicated father. I told her that we had a family and she needed to back off. She replied that she loved Kevin and was not going to stop seeing him. I confronted Kevin again after I spoke to the woman, and he no longer denied the affair. He just said, 'What do you want me to do?' Then he hung up on me. I had always held out hope that he would change, but at that moment I finally realized that he was never going to change. My marriage was over. My nightmare was coming true. And I felt worthless. It was the lowest point of my life."

Susan soon filed for divorce, and Kevin did not contest it. "He just walked away like we never existed." The divorce was finalized just over a year ago. Susan says that Kevin has visited the children sporadically. "He comes around maybe once every couple of months. My four-year-old son has no relationship with his father. My nine-year-old daughter longs to know her father. She gets so excited when she knows he is coming to visit, only to be disappointed by his lack of interest and affection. She has problems expressing her feelings as a result."

I asked Susan how the affair and divorce have affected her. Struggling to speak through a flood of tears, she said, "It would have been better if he had died during a mission. At least then we could have moved on. Right now I'm just existing—nothing more. I'm depressed and angry. This has changed my view of God. My faith has been shaken. I can't pray anymore. I haven't had a quiet time in six months. I now see God as cold and distant. To me God seems more interested in furthering his kingdom than in concerning himself with the problems in my life. Kevin did us wrong, and he walked away with no consequences. We are the ones who are suffering. Why would God allow that?"

SOMETHING BEAUTIFUL

When Carrie and Steve met in college, they quickly became close friends. They were both involved in Campus Crusade, seeking a closer relationship with God during a time when many young adults begin to drift from their faith. Steve struggled with homosexual thoughts and feelings. He was actually very open about that struggle, sharing it with his sister and with Carrie and with many other Christian friends. Though he had never acted on his thoughts and feelings, Steve considered them to be wrong and struggled to suppress them.

After graduation, Steve went to medical school in Texas, and Carrie entered a graduate program in California. Yet they remained close friends, corresponding regularly. After finishing medical school, Steve took a pediatric residency in Seattle. Carrie, still living in California, took advantage of their proximity to one another and drove to Seattle for a visit. After being friends for ten years, during that visit Steve and Carrie began to recognize that they were romantically attracted to each other. They began dating soon after that, and four months later they were engaged to be married.

As they prepared for their upcoming wedding, they discussed Steve's ongoing struggles with homosexual thoughts and feelings. Having received some counseling while in medical school, Steve assured Carrie that there was no problem. Steve told the pastor doing their premarital counseling about his struggles, and the pastor was not particularly concerned. Wanting to be absolutely sure that she wasn't making a mistake, Carrie sought counsel from a Christian couple who did marital counseling; and they also were not concerned. She talked to their mutual friends and to her own close friends, and none of them seemed to be overly concerned. The only person who raised any doubts about them getting married in light of Steve's struggles was a woman who had mentored and discipled Carrie. Steve's continued openness about his struggles and the assurance of so many strong believers gave Carrie peace as their wedding day neared. One year after getting engaged, Carrie and Steve were married.

Steve still had a year to go in his residency, so Carrie moved to Seattle. Much to the couple's surprise, Carrie had become pregnant on their honeymoon. The first year of their marriage was very difficult for Carrie. Because of the responsibilities of his residency, Steve was seldom home. Pregnant and alone in a new city, and with few friends and no family, Carrie began to sink into a dark depression, which only got worse after the birth of their daughter. As she struggled with postpartum depression and the responsibilities of being a new wife and mother, Carrie found herself overcome by anger and bitterness.

Once Steve completed his residency, he found a position in Texas. A new job, in a different state, was the fresh start the young couple needed. They quickly connected with a local church, and Steve started meeting with an accountability group of several men. With Steve home more and a growing support system of new friends, Carrie saw her depression gradually lift. "Our marriage was growing better and stronger. About two years after we moved to Texas, our son was born. It was around that same time that Steve started talking about us going to Africa."

Years earlier, when he was in medical school, Steve had traveled to Africa on a medical mission trip; and that experience had impacted him significantly. The couple asked their church and other friends to pray for them as they sought God's will for their future. Carrie remembers having a number of conversations with Steve about the potential problems that life on the mission field would bring to their family. Nevertheless, the couple eventually moved forward with plans to go to Africa.

Steve signed on with a missionary organization that places physicians overseas to train local doctors and nurses for Christian service. Preparation and training with the organization took about a year. Part of that preparation included an evaluation of Steve and Carrie's spiritual lives and marriage. Steve was open about his past struggles with homosexual thoughts and feelings, and Carrie shared about her problems with depression. Because those involved in assessing the couple were concerned about Carrie's potential for depression, they insisted that when she arrived in Africa she make contact with a local counseling center run by the missionary organization. The thinking was that this would provide her with support in the event that her depression returned. Steve's struggle with homosexual thoughts and feelings was not considered a problem, so nothing additional was required of him.

"After nine months in Africa," Carrie recalls, "Steve started having trouble again with homosexual thoughts and feelings. While he was open with me about his struggle, I don't think he really felt like he had anyone to talk to like he did back home. When you're a missionary, it's hard to be real with people. You're so concerned about what others think, about the image of the organization. It can be lonely. The more Steve struggled, the more angry he got with God. He would say, 'I feel like I've done everything God wanted me to do. Why hasn't he taken this away from me?' For six months I begged him to go to the counseling center and talk to someone."

During their second year in Africa, Steve decided to attend a medical conference in Denver. Because of his ongoing struggles, Carrie was not supportive of Steve making the trip; so she asked him not to go. Against his wife's wishes, Steve flew to Denver. There, in the exercise room of his hotel, a man propositioned Steve; and for the first time in his life he acted on the homosexual thoughts and feelings he had struggled so long to suppress.

"When Steve came back from Denver, he was a mess. He was nonfunctional and explosive. He would blow up at the kids or me for no reason. He didn't tell me about his sexual liaison, but he did say that every man he looked at brought a flood of sexual thoughts and feelings that he was almost unable to control. At that point I decided that if he wasn't going to go talk to someone, then I would. I went to the local counseling center, and they suggested that we go to a residential counseling center in California specifically for missionaries. When I told Steve, he was excited about the opportunity; so we began to make preparations to move."

Steve and Carrie were in the middle of adopting a young African boy who had been living with them for nine months. The government paperwork that would allow the child to travel to the United States with the family would take a month to process. Against Carrie's wishes, Steve decided to go to California ahead of the family in order to start counseling. Once there, Steve did begin counseling; but he also started pursuing the local homosexual community. Within a short time, he had become sexually involved with several men. By the time Carrie and the children arrived, Steve had decided to practice an openly homosexual lifestyle. He told Carrie about what had happened in Denver and about his homosexual activity since coming to California.

"I told him that, despite everything that had happened, I was still willing to work on the marriage if he was committed to the relationship. He said he was, but he also suggested that we separate for a period of time. I told him that was fine, as long as he understood that while we were separated we would agree not to see other people. He responded that he couldn't agree to that. So I took the children, moved back home to Texas, and filed for divorce a week later."

Steve later moved to Texas as well, to a city about two hours away. In the months following their separation, Steve became consumed with the homosexual lifestyle. "He was like a fifteen-year-old child, only concerned about himself. Our home church reached out to him, but he would have none of it. When I asked him how he could reconcile his homosexual lifestyle with his faith, he just said, 'I don't really care anymore what God thinks! I can't reconcile it, so I'm going to do what I want to do.'" Later that year, the divorce was finalized.

That was six years ago. Today Steve and Carrie have little contact other than through their children. "The children visit Steve every two weeks, so it is never all over for us. Steve has had a committed partner for the last two years, and that has brought a lot of stability to his life."

When I asked Carrie how she has been changed by these difficult trials, she replied, "They have made me a more compassionate person. I also have a better appreciation of God's faithfulness. He was always there. I am proof that when everything comes apart, the Lord can help you put your life back together again. He can take the broken pieces and make them into something beautiful."

FINAL THOUGHTS

I am so grateful to these three women who opened their hearts and shared their lives. I hope their stories have put a more personal face on the devastating effects of sin. It is important to understand that all three men in these stories openly professed Christ as Savior at some time in their lives, yet they were drawn away—enticed by their own lusts and desires. They chose the pleasures of sin over their wives, children, and faith.

These stories demonstrate that sin is an ever-present problem even in the church today. It is time that we, the body of Christ, move away from the "us versus the world" mentality. This mindset has crippled our ministry to the world and to one another. Instead, we need to seek to develop a truly transparent and open community of faith, fully dependent on the transforming power of Christ. In such a community, men and women do not struggle in silence with sinful lusts and desires but openly share and confess (James 5:16) to a body willing to carry one another's burdens (Galatians 6:1–2).

Chapter 9

Biology Is Not Destiny

Such were some of you.
—1 Corinthians 6:11

As a faculty member in the Baylor Addiction Research Center (BARC), I recently had the privilege of speaking to a local Celebrate Recovery group. Celebrate Recovery is an international Christ-centered recovery program that offers a safe place for people to find freedom from life's "hurts, hang-ups and habits." The evening began with worship, followed by the corporate reading of eight recovery principles, based on the Beatitudes from Jesus' Sermon on the Mount, and a prayer. While this may sound similar to many church meetings you have attended, what was different was that those who led introduced themselves something like this: "Hello! I'm John, and I'm a believer who struggles with pride, lust, and addiction to drugs." They were completely transparent about their struggles with sin, and they confidently recognized who they are in the eyes of God. They are believers, saints who struggle with sin and the problems of the world. They don't allow themselves to be identified merely by their sinful habits and behaviors but recognize that their true identity rests in Christ alone. The feeling of love and acceptance in the room was palpable. The air was electric with the anticipation of lives being transformed.

As I stood before the group to make my presentation, I thought, *This is what the church, the body of Christ, is supposed to be—broken, humble, and dependent. This was the church written about in Acts that we so long to know. This was Rome, Corinth, and Galatia.* The presence of God in the room was overwhelming. I had come to encourage them, but I was the one who was changed. My talk began differently than I had planned that night. The words were easier to say than I could have imagined. As I spoke them, I felt no fear, no condemnation—only the all-surpassing peace of God. "Hello! I'm Matt, and I'm a believer who struggles with . . ."

THE PERVASIVENESS OF SIN

My hope is that this book has challenged your perspective on sin, causing you to recognize sin as a spiritual phenomenon that also has a physical manifestation. Though we in the church talk tough about sin, I believe our actions are not consistent with our words. We talk like sinful behavior is easy to overcome, but the reality is that sin is pervasive and deeply ingrained in us. A few Bible verses and a quick prayer are not going to result in a life of sinless perfection. While we recognize that God calls us to be holy (a standard we like to hold others, rather than ourselves, to), we forget that Jesus has told us that we can do nothing apart from him (John 15:5). So we advise our brothers and sisters in the church to suppress and/or avoid sinful lusts and desires in an attempt to be godly. Unfortunately, this works-based approach to behavior change ultimately results in frustration and failure.

Christ isn't interested in just cleaning us up. He wants to completely transform us, recreating us in his likeness. Richard Foster describes the process this way: "The Christian message is not the elimination of desire but the transformation of desire. The overcoming of destructive desire and developing the inward reality of right desire is what we are after and what we can experience as our life is soaked in Jesus and his way."[105]

To be "soaked in Jesus" doesn't sound like a list of dos and don'ts, but rather an intimate and growing relationship with the giver of life. As we grow in intimacy with Jesus, we become more and more aware, as John Piper says, that "the power of sin is the false promise that it will bring more happiness than holiness will bring. . . . Therefore, what breaks the power of sin is faith in the true promise that the pleasures of sin are passing and poisonous, but at God's right hand are pleasures forevermore (Psalm 16:11)."[2]

BIOLOGY, SIN, AND THE BIBLE

The ancient Hebrews and the first-century Christians were unaware of how the brain and nervous system function. They were not unaware, however, that biology played a significant role in thoughts and behavior (e.g., Jeremiah 17:10; Psalm 26:2, 73:21–22).[3] They understood that disease or injury to the body could result in dramatic behavioral changes and physical manifestations, many of which are mentioned both in the biblical text (e.g., 2 Kings 4:18–20 appears to describe a subarachnoid hemorrhage in a child) and in other ancient writings, such as the Talmud (a record of Jewish laws and traditions).[4] It is also clear that the biblical writers understood that we struggle to control deeply ingrained, biologically related sinful impulses. The Scriptures make several references to these inborn sinful patterns and our attempts to bring them under control.

Peter suggests that those who indulge in such "fleshly lusts" and "corrupt desires" behave like unreasoning animals driven by instinct (1 Peter 2:11; 2 Peter 2:10–18). Jesus, when challenged by the Pharisees in relation to ceremonial cleanliness and the food laws, taught that defilement comes "from within, out of the heart," where sinful thoughts and behaviors originate (Matthew 15:19; Mark 7:21). John teaches us that the "lust of the flesh" is not of God and should not be pursued (1 John 2:16), while James instructs that the source of temptation is the innate lusts within each of us (James 1:14–15). Paul mentions these same fleshly patterns of lust and desire throughout his epistles (Romans 7:17–18, 23; 1 Corinthians 7:9; Galatians 5:16; Ephesians 2:3; 1 Thessalonians 4:5), describing them as overpowering and difficult to control (Romans 7:18–19; Galatians 5:17).

Biology, however, is not destiny. When we fully understand the effects of original sin on our physical bodies, it becomes clear that broken biology can never be used as an excuse for sinful behavior. Biblical scholar Robert Gagnon says it this way: "A biology-equals-morality rationale has no place in a worldview that talks of denying oneself, losing one's life, taking up one's cross, dying with Christ, new creation, and living for God."[5] The fact that we have sinful DNA is simply another example of why we so desperately need a Savior with the power to completely re-create us. We have been made new spiritually (2 Corinthians 5:17), and ultimately we will be transformed physically (1 Corinthians 15:53; Philippians 3:20–21).

WHEN SIN IS CALLED DISORDER

Christians often ask me if sin can be considered a disorder. Those who ask this question typically want to know if behavior associated with psychiatric disorders (for which there may or may not be a treatment) can be considered sinful or wrong. Of the behaviors I have chosen to highlight in earlier chapters, many presently are (rage, lying/stealing, addiction) or at one time were (homosexuality) associated with specific psychiatric disorders. But does calling a behavior that the Bible considers sinful a "disorder" somehow make that behavior no longer sin? Absolutely not!

In the context of medicine, a disorder is a condition in which there is a disturbance of normal functioning. To be disordered is to be broken, thrown into a state of disarray or confusion. In no way does labeling a behavior as disordered cause one to assume that the behavior is normal or accepted. In fact, just the opposite is true: disordered behavior is abnormal and implies the need for change. Sinful behavior, like all behavior, represents a complex interplay between physical (biological), mental, and spiritual factors. I find that the choice of label—"disorder" or "sin"—often results from one's perspective. If one focuses on the external or physical (biological), ignoring the spiritual, then one may call an abnormal behavior a disorder, while a focus on internal or spiritual aspects may result in the same behavior being labeled as sin. One label does not somehow change or limit the other; both describe the same behavior from different vantage points or perspectives.

The labeling of a behavior as both a sin and a disorder also results from the availability of effective treatments or interventions that temper or limit the expression of the problem behavior. Given that all behavior is rooted in biology, it is understandable that some sinful behaviors (e.g., addiction) can be altered through the use of physical remedies. The fact that there is such an overlap between behaviors considered disordered and those considered sinful is further proof that biological and spiritual factors are involved. Having said this, it is important to realize that while some sins may rightly be thought of as disorders, not all disordered behaviors (e.g., schizophrenia) are sin.

LOVE THE SINNER; HATE THE SIN

"Love the sinner; hate the sin." That statement certainly sounds good, and in a very real sense that is what we are supposed to do. But I have found, unfortunately, that what is more commonly practiced in the church today is "Judge the sinner; hate the sin." Even more disconcerting is the fact that we only have this attitude about a few select sins, such as addiction or homosexuality. Although we rank sins by how serious we believe them to be (e.g., homosexuality being worse than pride), the fact is that, apart from Christ, any sin disqualifies us from life with God (James 2:10).

I often use the following scenario to show people how we almost unconsciously treat sinful behaviors differently.

Imagine that you are a small-group leader in your church. One evening a couple that has just recently begun attending the church visits your small group. During the meeting you learn that both of them were brought up in Christian homes but over the course of many years have drifted away from their faith. Feeling that something has always been missing, they are now coming back to the church and seeking to reestablish a relationship with Christ. As the meeting ends and people begin to leave, you find out that the couple are not married, though they have been living together for several years. As the small-group leader, when do you think it would be appropriate to have a conversation with them about their living arrangement?

Virtually 100 percent of the Christians I have presented this scenario to have said that they would first build a relationship with the couple before talking with them about their living arrangement. By most estimates that would occur over several weeks or months. Showing this couple the love and acceptance of Christ before a discussion of specific sin in their lives has been emphasized by everyone to whom I have spoken.

Now imagine a similar small-group scenario, but this time the couple consists of two homosexual men. The most common response to this situation is stunned silence followed by what we in the South call "a bunch of hem-hawing around." Most Christians I have talked with about this scenario have had to painfully admit that the homosexual couple would be approached almost immediately in regard to their sin and not welcomed back into the group until their behavior changed.

Why do we see these couples so differently? Both couples are seeking to reestablish a relationship with Christ, and both are involved in sexual immorality. My question to the church is, *Are they different?* Please don't misunderstand me. I'm not saying that we should ignore or minimize sinful behavior, but we should at least be consistent when dealing with individuals who are seeking a relationship with God.

When individuals come to faith in Christ, they certainly recognize their overall sinfulness and need for a Savior. But few, if any, recognize every specific sinful behavior in their lives. I have heard on many occasions the testimonies of longtime believers who had just recognized the presence of hidden sin in their lives. In those instances the revelation of unrecognized sin was praised as the continued work of the Holy Spirit in the life of the believer. Sanctification is a progressive process that occurs over a lifetime, and we need to recognize that this is true for all sin. People should never be given the impression that they need to clean themselves up before they come to Christ, since their sins are somehow worse than the sins of others. We must be prepared to share the love of Christ with everyone, particularly with those who are seeking a deeper relationship with the giver of life.

A BATTLE OF THE MIND

Since who we are in Christ is at odds with our most innate impulses and desires (Romans 8:5–8), we have been called to deny our flesh and follow Jesus (Matthew 16:24; Mark 8:34; Luke 9:23). This conflict between who we are in Christ and our fleshly lusts and desires occurs in the mind (Romans 8:5–7; Colossians 3:1–8). Satan takes full advantage of this mental conflict to blind the minds of the lost to the transforming power of the gospel (2 Corinthians 4:4) and to lead the saints astray to follow after their own selfish drives and impulses (2 Corinthians 11:3).

When ministering to those caught up in sin who do not know the Lord, the gospel must always be the primary emphasis (Romans 1:16), since it is only through the transforming power of the gospel that an individual has any hope of being set free from bondage to sin (John 8:32). When our brothers and sisters in the Lord fall into sin, the Scriptures call us to help restore them in a spirit of gentleness (Galatians 6:1). In either case, a transformation or renewing of the mind is the ultimate goal (Romans 12:2; Ephesians 4:20–24).

The first step in the process of renewing the mind is **submission**. The strength necessary to deny one's fleshly lusts and desires does not come from a strong will or right attitude. It comes through moment-by-moment dependence on Christ. Jesus says that we can do nothing apart from him (John 15:5), and that includes making a change in our behavior. God didn't ask you to save yourself, and he isn't asking you to sanctify yourself either. He simply wants you to submit to his indwelling Spirit and allow him to transform you into the image of his Son (2 Corinthians 3:18; James 4:7; 1 Peter 5:6). The Scriptures tell us that the very power that raised Christ from the dead is presently working in us (Ephesians 1:19–20). It is only through that resurrection power that a transformation of sinful desires is possible.

The second step in renewal is **setting or preparing the mind**. Before we come to faith in Christ, our minds are directed toward only the flesh and the things of the world (Ephesians 4:17–19). Once we are transformed spiritually, we have a choice: we can choose whether to set our minds on the things of the flesh or on the things of the Spirit (Romans 8:5–7; Colossians 3:2). Through regular study of the Scriptures, prayer, and meditating on the things of the Lord, we prepare our minds for the temptations and distractions of the world that inevitably will come. As we make the setting of our minds a daily routine, then a godly mental focus becomes more and more of an unconscious habit. Preparing before temptations and trials come firmly grounds us in Christ, allowing us to weather the storms of life (Matthew 7:24–27).

The third step in the process of renewing our minds is **taking thoughts captive** (2 Corinthians 10:5). We can expect that sinful lusts and desires will rise up in us; temptations will come. What the adversary would use to destroy us, however, God can use to strengthen our faith and draw us closer to him (James 1:2–4). To be taken captive, sinful thoughts must first be recognized; and that is only possible if we have prepared our minds beforehand. As thoughts come to mind, they must be compared with and submitted to the mind of Christ, to which we have access through the indwelling Spirit (1 Corinthians 2:14–16). In every instance we must ask, "Is this how a child of the King, a coheir with Christ, should think or behave?" We can rest in the fact that God is sovereign over temptation. He will not allow you to be tempted beyond your ability to endure, no matter how overwhelming or irresistible the trial may seem (1 Corinthians 10:13).

Finally, we must form intimate and healthy relationships with other believers that give us the opportunity to **confess our sins** and hold one another accountable for our thoughts and actions (James 5:16; 1 John 1:9). Sin has power only when it is cloaked in darkness. Brought out into the light, sinful lusts and desires are quickly recognized for what they are: cheap imitations of true pleasure and happiness. The development of transparent relationships between believers that allows them a safe and accepting place to confess their shortcomings is integral in breaking the power of sin. If we are always walking in the light, then sinful lusts and desires are unlikely to find a foothold in our lives, and temptation can be quickly overcome (1 John 1:5–7).

FORGIVENESS

It is likely that many people reading this book have been hurt by friends and family members who are involved in the sinful behaviors discussed earlier. It is important for you to realize that their struggle with sinful behavior is just as much a test of your faith as it is theirs. God wants to use this situation to draw you into a closer and more intimate relationship with him.

While you can certainly support and encourage your friends and family members, you cannot fix them. One way you can encourage them is by expressing the transformative power of Christ to them through forgiveness. Forgiveness is agreeing to live with the consequences of another person's sin. The hard truth is that you are going to live with those consequences anyway, whether you like it or not. The choice you have to make is whether you will do so in bitterness or in freedom. The Scriptures are clear: our ability to forgive others is intimately associated with our spiritual health and growth (Matthew 6:14–15, 18:34–35; Mark 11:25). Holding on to unforgiveness is destructive only to you, not to the one who harmed you.

Forgiveness is a choice, an act of the will. Don't wait for the other person to ask for your forgiveness before you forgive. They may never do so. Don't wait to forgive until you feel like forgiving. It will always be painful and difficult, no matter how you feel. Ask God to give you the faith to forgive (Luke 17:3–5).

Remember that forgiving is not forgetting. While your act of forgiveness says that you no longer hold that person accountable for harming you, he or she is still accountable to God. Let your motivation for forgiving be the incarnate Son, who, even as he was being crucified, cried out for forgiveness to be given to his executioners (Luke 23:34).

FINAL THOUGHTS

A commonality shared by all the behaviors I have discussed in this book is that God calls them sin. Each behavior violates, in some way, the creative order he has established and thus is contrary to the will of the Creator. If you struggle with habitual sinful behavior, the most important thing for you to realize is that this is about you and about your relationship with Christ. It isn't about changing for another or conforming to a "religious" set of values. Change comes when we recognize that sin can never complete us the way Christ can. If you have tried to change in the past but have found yourself falling back into the same old sinful habits, realize that sanctification is progressive. If you have been saved by faith in Christ, then you are a holy, righteous child of God—regardless of how you may choose to behave at times. That said, your sinful choices do destroy the level of intimacy in your relationship with God.

Paul admonished the saints in the troubled church at Corinth to stop falling back into their old ways of behaving: "Do you not know that the unrighteous will not inherit the kingdom of God? Do not be deceived; neither fornicators, nor idolaters, nor adulterers, nor effeminate, nor homosexuals, nor thieves, nor the covetous, nor drunkards, nor revilers, nor swindlers, will inherit the kingdom of God. Such were some of you; but you were washed, but you were sanctified, but you were justified in the name of the Lord Jesus Christ and in the Spirit of our God" (1 Corinthians 6:9–11).

Did you see it? My favorite line in all of Scripture: *Such were some of you.* They had been changed. They didn't have to live the old way anymore. Real, lasting change through Christ was possible in the first century, and it is still possible today. Isn't it time you started living like a child of the King?

Appendix

Counseling and
Ministry Resources

CHRISTIAN MENTAL HEALTH COUNSELORS,
PSYCHOLOGISTS, AND PHYSICIANS

American Association of Christian Counselors (AACC)
PO Box 739
Forest, VA 24551
(800) 526-8673
www.aacc.net

Association of Biblical Counselors (ABC)
PO Box 126555
Fort Worth, TX 76126
(877) 222-4551
www.christiancounseling.com

Christian Association for Psychological Studies (CAPS)
PO Box 365
Batavia, IL 60510-0365
(630) 639-9478
www.caps.net

Christian Medical and Dental Associations (CMDA)
PO Box 7500
Bristol, TN 37621
(888) 230-2637
www.cmda.org

National Association of Nouthetic Counselors (NANC)
3600 W. 96th St.
Indianapolis, IN 46268
(317) 337-9100
www.nanc.org

Meier Clinics
(888) 7-CLINIC (725-4642)
www.meierclinics.com

ANGER AND VIOLENCE

National Organizations

National Domestic Violence Hotline
(800) 799-SAFE (7233)
www.ndvh.org

Stop Family Violence
331 W. 57th St. #518
New York, NY 10019
www.stopfamilyviolence.org

Ministries

Meier Clinics
(888) 7-CLINIC (725-4642)
www.meierclinics.com

New Life Ministries
PO Box 1018
Laguna Beach, CA 92652
(800) NEW-LIFE (639-5433)
www.newlife.com

Suggested Reading

Neil T. Anderson and Rich Miller, *Getting Anger under Control* (Eugene, OR: Harvest House, 2002)

Lundy Bancroft, *Why Does He Do That? Inside the Minds of Angry and Controlling Men* (New York: Berkley, 2003)

Gary Chapman, *Anger: Handling a Powerful Emotion in a Healthy Way* (Chicago: Northfield, 2007)

PORNOGRAPHY AND SEXUAL ADDICTION

National Organizations

COSA
International Service Organization of COSA
PO Box 14537
Minneapolis, MN 55414
(763) 537-6904
www.cosa-recovery.org

Sexual Addicts Anonymous (SAA)
International Service Organization of SAA
PO Box 70949
Houston, TX 77270
(800) 477-8191
www.sexaa.org

Ministries

Pure Life Ministries
14 School St.
Dry Ridge, KY 41035
(888) 787-3543
www.purelifeministries.org

Setting Captives Free
PO Box 1527
Medina, OH 44258-1527
(330) 620-8448
www.settingcaptivesfree.com

Suggested Reading

Stephen Arterburn and Fred Stoeker, *Every Man's Battle: Winning the War on Sexual Temptation One Victory at a Time* (Colorado Springs: WaterBrook, 2009)

Russell Willingham, *Breaking Free: Understanding Sexual Addiction and the Healing Power of Jesus* (Downers Grove, IL: InterVarsity, 1999)

Meg Wilson, *Hope after Betrayal: Healing When Sexual Addiction Invades Your Marriage* (Grand Rapids: Kregel, 2007)

MARITAL INFIDELITY

Ministries

FamilyLife
PO Box 7111
Little Rock, AR 72223
(800) FL-TODAY (358-6329)
www.familylife.com

New Life Ministries
PO Box 1018
Laguna Beach, CA 92652
(800) NEW-LIFE (639-5433)
www.newlife.com

Suggested Reading

Shirley P. Glass and Jean Coppock Staeheli, *Not "Just Friends": Rebuilding Trust and Recovering Your Sanity after Infidelity* (New York: Free Press, 2004)

Stephen M. Judah, *Staying Together When an Affair Pulls You Apart* (Downers Grove, IL: InterVarsity, 2006)

Gary Shriver and Mona Shriver, *Unfaithful: Rebuilding Trust after Infidelity* (Colorado Springs: David C. Cook, 2005)

CRIMINAL OFFENDERS AND EX-OFFENDERS

National Organizations

National H.I.R.E. Network
Legal Action Center
225 Varick St.
New York, NY 10014
(212) 243-1313
www.hirenetwork.org

The Salvation Army
www.salvationarmyusa.org

United Way
www.liveunited.org

Ministries

Billy Graham Center
Institute for Prison Ministries
500 College Ave.
Wheaton, IL 60187
(630) 752-5727
www.bgcprisonministries.com

Prison Fellowship
44180 Riverside Pkwy.
Lansdowne, VA 20176
(877) 478-0100
www.prisonfellowship.org

Suggested Reading

Natalie Berglund, *Out to Stay: A Look at Prison Recidivism* (Fairfax, VA: Xulon Press, 2002)

Jack Cranfield, Mark Victor Hansen, and Tom Lagana, *Chicken Soup for the Prisoner's Soul: 101 Stories to Open the Heart and Rekindle the Spirit of Hope, Healing and Forgiveness* (Deerfield Beach, FL: Health Communications, 2002)

Lennie Spitale, *Prison Ministry: Understanding Prison Culture Inside and Out* (Nashville, B & H Publishers, 2002)

ALCOHOL AND DRUG ADDICTION

National Organizations

Alcoholics Anonymous (AA)
PO Box 459
New York, NY 10163
(212) 870-3400
www.aa.org

Narcotics Anonymous (NA)
PO Box 9999
Van Nuys, CA 91409
(818) 773-9999
www.na.org

Substance Abuse and Mental Health Services Administration
(SAMHSA)
www.samhsa.gov
Substance Abuse Treatment Facility Locator
http://dasis3.samhsa.gov

Ministries

Celebrate Recovery
www.celebraterecovery.com

Suggested Reading

Neil T. Anderson and Mike and Julia Quarles, *Freedom from Addiction: Breaking the Bondage of Addiction and Finding Freedom in Christ* (Ventura, CA: Regal Books, 1996)

Gerald G. May, *Addiction and Grace: Love and Spirituality in the Healing of Addictions* (New York: HarperOne, 2007)

Edward T. Welch, *Addictions: A Banquet in the Grave: Finding Hope in the Power of the Gospel* (Phillipsburg, NJ: P & R Publishing, 2001)

HOMOSEXUALITY

National Organizations

National Association for Research and Therapy of Homosexuality
(NARTH)
307 W. 200 South, Suite 3001
Salt Lake City, UT 84101
(888) 364-4744
www.narth.com

Ministries

Desert Stream Ministries
706 Main St.
Grandview, MO 64030
(866) 359-0500
www.desertstream.org

Exodus International
PO Box 540119
Orlando, FL 32854
(407) 599-6872
www.exodus-international.org

Suggested Reading

Joe Dallas, *Desires in Conflict: Hope for Men Who Struggle with Sexual Identity* (Eugene, OR: Harvest House, 2003)

Janelle Hallman, *The Heart of Female Same-Sex Attraction: A Comprehensive Counseling Resource* (Downers Grove, IL: InterVarsity, 2008)

Francis MacNutt, *Can Homosexuality Be Healed?* (Grand Rapids: Chosen Books, 2006)

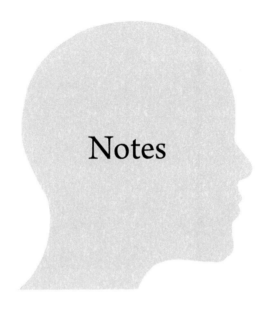

Notes

Chapter 1

1. Martin Luther, *Luther's Small Catechism* (St. Louis: Concordia, 1943), 86.

2. The Hebrew word for "man," *adam*, in Genesis 1:26 is a generic term covering both the male and female of the human species. The word, which has no plural form, does not refer exclusively to males. "Man" (*adam*) reflects the unity of all human beings. "Male and female" (Genesis 1:27) reflects the diversity of humankind. Both male and female are "man."

3. "FastStats: Life Expectancy," Centers for Disease Control and Prevention website, www.cdc.gov/nchs/fastats/lifexpec.htm.

4. In 1973 homosexuality was removed from the *Diagnostic and Statistical Manual of Mental Disorders* (DSM) and is no longer considered a mental illness by psychiatry and psychology.

5. Hidehiko Takahashi et al., "When your gain is my pain and your pain is my gain: Neural correlates of envy and schadenfreude," *Science* 323 (2009): 937–39.

6. "Two Sexes 'Sin in Different Ways,'" *BBC News*, February 18, 2009, http://news.bbc.co.uk/go/pr/fr/-/2/hi/europe/7897034.stm.

Chapter 2

1. Bill Gillham, *Lifetime Guarantee: Making Your Christian Life Work and What to Do When It Doesn't* (Eugene, OR: Harvest House, 1993), 17.

2. Donald K. Campbell, "Galatians," in *The Bible Knowledge Commentary: New Testament*, ed. John F. Walvoord and Roy B. Zuck (Wheaton: Victor), 607–8.

Chapter 3

1. I do not use men exclusively in my aggression studies, but in this particular study we were targeting men.

2. Office of Justice Programs, United States Department of Justice website (www.ojp.usdoj. gov), 2005 data.

3. Patricia Tjaden and Nancy Thoennes, National Institute of Justice, *Full Report of the Prevalence, Incidence, and Consequences of Violence against Women: Findings from the National Violence against Women Survey*, November 2000, www.ojp.usdoj.gov/nij/pubs-sum/183781. htm.

4. National Institute of Justice, "National Institute of Justice Update: Preventing Interpersonal Violence among Youths" (Washington, DC: U.S. Department of Justice, October 1994).

5. Emil F. Coccaro et al., "Lifetime and 1-month prevalence rates of intermittent explosive disorder in a community sample," *Journal of Clinical Psychiatry* 65 (2004): 820–24.

6. Matthew S. Stanford, Kevin. W. Greve, and Theodore J. Dickens, "Irritability and impulsiveness: Relationship to self-reported impulsive aggression," *Personality and Individual Differences* 19 (1995): 757–60; Maurizio Fava et al., "Anger attacks in depressed outpatients and their response to fluoxetine," *Psychopharmacology Bulletin* 27 (1991): 275–79.

7. Richard J. Davidson et al., "Dysfunction in the neural circuitry of emotion regulation—A possible prelude to violence," *Science* 289 (2000): 591–94.

8. Adrian Raine et al., "Selective reductions in prefrontal glucose metabolism in murderers," *Biological Psychiatry* 36 (1994): 365–73; Adrian Raine et al., "Reduced prefrontal and increased subcortical brain functioning assessed using positron emission tomography in predatory and affective murderers," *Behavioral Sciences and the Law* 16 (1998): 319–32; Emil F. Coccaro et al., "Amygdala and orbitofrontal reactivity to social threat in individuals with impulsive aggression," *Biological Psychiatry* 62 (2007): 168–78.

9. Emil F. Coccaro et al., "Heritability of irritable impulsiveness: A study of twin pairs reared together and apart," *Psychiatry Research* 51 (1993): 318–24; Emil F. Coccaro et al., "Heritability of aggression and irritability: A twin study of the Buss-Durkee aggression scales in adult male subjects," *Biological Psychiatry* 41 (1997): 273–84.

10. Donna R. Miles and Gregory Carey, "Genetic and environmental architecture of human aggression," *Journal of Personality and Social Psychology*, 72 (1997): 207–217.

11. Dan Rujescu et al., "Association of anger-related traits with SNPs in the TPH gene," *Molecular Psychiatry* 7 (2002): 1023–29; Wolfgang Retz et al., "Association of serotonin transporter promoter gene polymorphism with violence: Relation with personality disorders, impulsivity and childhood ADHD psychopathology," *Behavioral Sciences and the Law* 22 (2004): 415–25.

12. Other impulsive behaviors include promiscuous sex, substance abuse, binge eating, driving recklessly, shoplifting, and going on spending sprees.

13. American Psychiatric Association, *Diagnostic and Statistical Manual of Mental Disorders*, 4th ed., text revision (Washington, DC: American Psychiatric Association, 2000), 663–67.

14. For a discussion of the difference between men and women in regard to sin, see the "Why Men?" section in chapter 1.

15. Antonia S. New et al., "Fluoxetine increases relative metabolic rate in prefrontal cortex in impulsive aggression," *Psychopharmacology* 176 (2004): 451–58.

16. Matthew S. Stanford et al., "A comparison of anticonvulsants in the treatment of impulsive aggression," *Experimental and Clinical Psychopharmacology* 13 (2005): 72–77; Matthew S. Stanford et al., "A double-blind placebo-controlled crossover study of Phenytoin in individuals with impulsive aggression," *Psychiatry Research* 103 (2001): 193–203.

17. For a more detailed discussion of these disorders, see my book *Grace for the Afflicted: A Clinical and Biblical Perspective on Mental Illness* (Colorado Springs: Paternoster, 2008).

18. Gary Chapman, *Anger: Handling a Powerful Emotion in a Healthy Way* (Chicago: Northfield Publishing, 2007), 26.

19. Ibid., 19.

Chapter 4

1. *Strong's Exhaustive Concordance of the Bible*, Hebrew Dictionary, s.v. *na'aph* (entry 5003).

2. Jerry Ropelato, "Internet Pornography Statistics (2006)," TopTenREVIEWS, http://internet-filter-review.toptenreviews.com/internet-pornography-statistics.html.

3. Ibid.

4. David Atkins and Deborah E. Kessel, "Religiousness and infidelity: Attendance, but not faith and prayer, predict marital fidelity," *Journal of Marriage and Family* 70 (2008): 407–18; Adrian J. Blow and Kelley Hartnett, "Infidelity in committed relationships II: A substantive review," *Journal of Marital and Family Therapy* 31 (2005): 217–34. For a discussion of the difference between men and women in regard to sin, see the "Why Men?" section in chapter 1.

5. Durex, "The Global Sex Survey (2005)," available at http://www.durex.com.

6. In some instances God calls individuals to a life of celibacy (Matthew 19:10–12; 1 Corinthians 7:1–9, 32–35) so that they may be able to devote themselves completely to ministry. Empowered by the Holy Spirit, they are able to maintain control over their sexual impulses/desires and voluntarily remain single without regret. Celibacy is a state totally opposed to all of the biological and emotional needs built into a man or woman by God.

7. Devra Kleiman, "Monogamy in mammals," *Quarterly Review of Biology* 52 (1977): 36–69.

8. Helen E. Fisher, "Evolution of human serial pairbonding," *American Journal of Physical Anthropology* 78 (1989): 331–54.

9. Theresa L. Crenshaw, *The Alchemy of Love and Lust: How Our Sex Hormones Influence Our Relationships* (New York: Pocket Books, 1996), 164–202.

10. Andreas Bartels and Semir Zeki, "The neural basis of love," *Neuroreport* 11 (2000): 3829–34; Arthur Aron et al., "Reward, motivation and emotion systems associated with early-stage intense romantic love," *Journal of Neurophysiology* 94 (2005): 327–37.

11. Helen Fisher, *Why We Love: The Nature and Chemistry of Romantic Love* (New York: Henry Holt, 2004), 170.

12. C. Sue Carter, "Neuroendocrine perspectives on social attachment and love," *Psychoneuroendocrinology* 23 (1998): 779–818.

13. Helen E. Fisher et al., "Defining the brain systems of lust, romantic attraction and attachment," *Archives of Sexual Behavior* 31 (2002): 413–19.

14. A. Wayne Meikle et al., "Quantitating genetic and nongenetic factors influencing androgen production and clearance rates in men," *Journal of Clinical Endocrinology Metabolism* 67 (1988): 104–9.

15. Alan Booth and James M. Dabbs Jr., "Testosterone and men's marriages," *Social Forces* 72 (1993): 463–77.

16. Janice Shaw Crouse, "Love Potion Number 'O,'" Beverly LaHaye Institute, January, 19, 2006, www.beverlylahayeinstitute.org/articledisplay.asp?id=9936&department=BLI&categoryid=dotcommentary&subcategoryid=blicul.

17. Dirk H. Hellhammer, Walter Hubert, and Thomas Schurmeyer, "Changes in saliva testosterone after psychological stimulation in men," *Psychoneuroendocrinology* 10 (1985): 77–81; Alison Motluk, "How pornography turns women on too," *New Scientist* 2148 (1998): 11.

18. Robert Ellis, Marketplace Ministry, Grand Rapids, MI, www.marketplaceministry.org, personal communication.

19. Stephen Arterburn, *Addicted to "Love": Understanding Dependencies of the Heart: Romance, Relationships, and Sex* (Ann Arbor, MI: Vine Books, 1996), 112.

Chapter 5

1. Roy Walmsley, "World Prison Population List (eighth edition)," 2008, available at International Centre for Prison Studies, King's College London website, www.kcl.ac.uk/depsta/law/research/icps/downloads/wppl-8th_41.pdf; Crime in the United States, 2008, Federal Bureau of Investigation website, www.fbi.gov/ucr/cius2008/index.html; The Bureau of Justice Statistics, http://bjs.ojp.usdoj.gov/index.cfm?ty=tp&tid=11.

2. Kristen A. Hughes, "Justice Expenditures and Employment in the United States, 2003," available at U.S. Department of Justice website, www.ojp.usdoj.gov/bjs/pub/pdf/jeeus03.pdf.

3. David A. Anderson, "The aggregate burden of crime," *Journal of Law and Economics* 42 (1999): 611–42.

4. James R. P. Ogloff, "Psychopathy/antisocial personality disorder conundrum," *Australian and New Zealand Journal of Psychiatry* 40 (2006): 519–28.

5. American Psychiatric Association, *Diagnostic and Statistical Manual of Mental Disorders,* 4th ed., text revision (Washington, DC: American Psychiatric Association, 2000).

6. For a more detailed discussion of borderline personality disorder, see my book *Grace for the Afflicted: A Clinical and Biblical Perspective on Mental Illness* (Colorado Springs: Paternoster, 2008).

7. Mark F. Lenzenweger et al., "DSM-IV personality disorders in the national comorbidity survey replication," *Biological Psychiatry* 62 (2007): 553–64.

8. Roel Verheul, Louisa M. C. van den Bosch, and Samuel A. Ball, "Substance Abuse"; in John M. Oldham, Andrew E. Skodol, and Donna S. Bender, eds., *Textbook of Personality Disorders* (Washington, DC: American Psychiatric Association, 2005), 463–76.

9. For a discussion of the difference between men and women in regard to sin, see the "Why Men?" section in chapter 1.

10. American Psychiatric Association, *Diagnostic and Statistical Manual of Mental Disorders,* 701–6.

11. Sharon S. Ishikawa and Adrian Raine, "Psychophysiological correlates of antisocial behavior: A central control hypothesis"; in Joseph Glicksohn, ed., *The Neurobiology of Criminal Behavior* (Boston: Kluwer Academic Publishers, 2002), 187–229.

12. Adrian Raine, Peter H. Venables, and Mark Williams, "Relationship between central autonomic measures of arousal at age 15 years and criminality at age 24 years," *Archives of General Psychiatry* 47 (1990): 1003–7.

13. Lindley Bassarath, "Neuroimaging studies of antisocial behavior," *Canadian Journal of Psychiatry* 46 (2001): 728–32. Adrian Raine et al., "Reduced prefrontal gray matter volume and

reduced autonomic activity in antisocial personality disorder," *Archives of General Psychiatry* 57 (2000): 119–27.

14. Henrik Soderstrom et al., "Reduced frontotemporal perfusion in psychopathic personality," *Psychiatry Research: Neuroimaging* 114 (2002): 81–94.

15. Adrian Raine, *The Psychopathology of Crime: Criminal Behavior as a Clinical Disorder* (San Diego: Academic Press, 1993), 55–58; Terri E. Moffitt, "The new look of behavioral genetics in developmental psychopathology: Gene-environment interplay in antisocial behavior," *Psychological Bulletin* 131 (2005): 533–54.

16. Raine, *Psychopathology of Crime*, 59–62.

17. Lee Ellis, "A theory explaining biological correlates of criminality," *European Journal of Criminology* 2 (2005): 287–315.

18. Emil F. Coccaro et al., "Serotonergic studies in patients with affective and personality disorders," *Archives of General Psychiatry* 46 (1989): 587–99; Royce Lee and Emil F. Coccaro, "The neuropharmacology of criminality and aggression," *Canadian Journal of Psychiatry* 46 (2001): 35–44.

19. Mordechai Rotenberg and Bernard L. Diamond, "The biblical conception of psychopathy: The law of the stubborn and rebellious son," *Journal of the History of the Behavioral Sciences* 7 (1971): 29–38.

20. Elizabeth Bellefontaine, "Deuteronomy 21:18–21: Reviewing the case of the rebellious son," *Journal for the Study of the Old Testament* 13 (1979): 21.

Chapter 6

1. Patrick E. McGovern et al., "Fermented beverages of pre- and proto-historic China," *Proceedings of the National Academy of Sciences* 101 (2004): 17593–98.

2. Substance Abuse and Mental Health Services Administration, "Results from the 2007 National Survey on Drug Use and Health: National Findings" (Rockville, MD: Office of Applied Studies, NSDUH Series H-34, DHHS Publication No. SMA 08-4343, 2008).

3. For a discussion of the difference between men and women in regard to sin, see the "Why Men?" section in chapter 1.

4. Schneider Institute for Health Policy, *Substance Abuse: The Nation's Number One Health Problem* (Princeton, NJ: The Robert Wood Johnson Foundation, 2001).

5. Russil Durrant and Jo Thakker, *Substance Use and Abuse: Cultural and Historical Perspectives* (Thousand Oaks, CA: Sage Publications, 2003), 193–94.

6. Luis Hernandez and Bartley G. Hoebel, "Food reward and cocaine increase extracellular dopamine in the nucleus accumbens as measured by microdialysis," *Life Sciences* 42 (1988): 1705–12.

7. Kenneth Blum et al., "Reward Deficiency Syndrome: Neurobiological and Genetic Aspects"; in Kenneth Blum et al. (eds.), *Handbook of Psychiatric Genetics* (Boca Raton, FL: CRC Press, 1997) 407–32.

8. Kenneth Blum et al., "The D2 Dopamine Gene as a Determinant of Reward Deficiency Syndrome," *Journal of the Royal Academy of Medicine* 89 (1996): 396–400.

9. Substance Abuse and Mental Health Services Administration, "Results from the 2007 National Survey." Survey respondents could indicate that they received treatment for more than one substance during their most recent treatment, so there is some overlap in the numbers.

10. John W. Finney, Annette C. Hahn, and Rudolf H. Moos, "The effectiveness of inpatient and outpatient treatment for alcohol abuse: The need to focus on mediators and moderators of setting effects," *Addiction* 91 (1996): 1773–96.

11. J. Michael Polich, David J. Armor, and Harriet B. Braiker, *The Course of Alcoholism: Four Years after Treatment* (New York: John Wiley & Sons, 1981), 159–200.

12. Edward T. Welch, *Blame It on the Brain? Distinguishing Chemical Imbalances, Brain Disorders, and Disobedience* (Phillipsburg, NJ: P & R Publishing, 1998), 192–94.

Chapter 7

1. Dan O. Via and Robert A. J. Gagnon, *Homosexuality and the Bible: Two Views* (Minneapolis: Fortress Press, 2003), 40.

2. John Young, "Guided by His Bible, He Embraced His Gay Son," *Waco Tribune-Herald*, editorial page, December 14, 2008.

3. Alfred C. Kinsey, Wardell B. Pomeroy, and Clyde Martin, *Sexual Behavior in the Human Male* (Philadelphia: W. B. Saunders, 1948), 651.

4. Stanton L. Jones and Mark A. Yarhouse, *Homosexuality: The Use of the Scientific Research in the Church's Moral Debate* (Downers Grove, IL: InterVarsity, 2000).

5. Paul H. Gebhard, "Incidence of Overt Homosexuality in the United States and Western Europe," in *National Institute of Mental Health Task Force on Homosexuality: Final Report and Background Papers*, ed. J. M. Livingood (Rockville, MD: National Institute of Mental Health, 1972).

6. For a discussion of the difference between men and women in regard to sin, see the "Why Men?" section in chapter 1.

7. Qazi Rahman and Glen D. Wilson, "Born gay? The psychobiology of human sexual orientation," *Personality and Individual Differences* 24 (2003): 1337–82.

8. Dick F. Swaab and Michel A. Hofman, "An enlarged suprachiasmatic nucleus in homosexual men," *Brain Research* 537 (1990): 141–48.

9. Simon LeVay, "A difference in hypothalamic structure between heterosexual and homosexual men," *Science* 253 (1991): 1034–37; William Byne et al., "The interstitial nuclei of the human anterior hypothalamus: An investigation of variation with sex, sexual orientation and HIV status," *Hormones and Behavior* 40 (2001): 86–92.

10. Alicia Gracia-Falgueras and Dick F. Swaab, "A sex difference in the hypothalamic uncinate nucleus: Relationship to gender identity," *Brain* 131 (2008): 3132–46.

11. Charles E. Roselli et al., "Sexual partner preference, hypothalamic morphology and aromatase in rams," *Physiology and Behavior* 83 (2004): 233–45.

12. Dick F. Swaab et al., "Increased number of vasopressin neurons in the suprachiasmatic nucleus (SCN) of 'bisexual' adult male rats following perinatal treatment with the aromatase blocker ATD," *Developmental Brain Research* 85 (1995): 273–79.

13. Roselli et al., "Sexual partner preference," 233–45.

14. Melissa Hines et al., "Testosterone during pregnancy and gender role behavior of preschool children: A longitudinal, population study," *Child Development* 73 (2002): 1678–87; J. Richard Udry et al., "Androgen effects on women's gender behavior," *Journal of Biosocial Science* 27 (1995): 359–68.

15. Catherine M. Hall et al., "Behavioral and physical masculinization are related to genotype in girls with congenital adrenal hyperplasia," *Journal of Clinical Endocrinology and Metabolism* 89 (2004): 419–24.

16. Heino F. L. Meyer-Bahlburg et al., "Sexual orientation in women with classical or nonclassical congenital adrenal hyperplasia as a function of degree of prenatal androgen excess," *Archives of Sexual Behavior* 37 (2008): 85–99.

17. Rahman and Wilson, "Born gay?" 1341–43.

18. Dean H. Hamer, "Genetics and male sexual orientation," *Science* 285 (1999): 803.

19. American Psychiatric Association, *Diagnostic and Statistical Manual of Mental Disorders*, 4th ed., text revision (Washington, DC: American Psychiatric Association, 2000), 582.

20. Robert Epstein, "Smooth Thinking about Sexuality," *Scientific American Mind*, October–November 2007, 14.

21. Joseph Nicolosi et al., "Retrospective self-reports of change in homosexual orientation: A consumer survey of conversion therapy clients," *Psychological Reports* 86 (2000): 1071–88; Warren Throckmorton, "Initial empirical and clinical findings concerning the change process

for ex-gays," *Professional Psychology: Research and Practice* 33 (2002): 242–48; Ariel Shidlo and Michael Schroeder, "Changing sexual orientation: A consumers' report," *Professional Psychology: Research and Practice* 33 (2002): 249–59; A. Dean Byrd and Joseph Nicolosi, "A meta-analytic review of treatment of homosexuality," *Psychological Reports* 90 (2002): 1139–52; Robert L. Spitzer, "Can some gay men and lesbians change their sexual orientation? 200 participants reporting a change from homosexual to heterosexual orientation," *Archives of Sexual Behavior* 32 (2003): 403–17; Stanton L. Jones and Mark A. Yarhouse, *Ex-Gays? A Longitudinal Study of Religiously Mediated Change in Sexual Orientation* (Downers Grove, IL: InterVarsity, 2007).

22. Quoted by Warren Throckmorton in "Did Jesus Bless Homosexuality?" November 1, 2005; available on the Concerned Women for America website, www.cwfa.org/articles/9355/CFI/family/index.htm.

23. Faris Malik, "The Ancient Roman and Talmudic Definition of Natural Eunuchs" (paper presented at Cardiff University, Cardiff, Wales, July 27, 1999); available at www.well.com/user/aquarius/cardiff.htm.

24. R. Albert Mohler Jr., *Desire and Deceit: The Real Cost of the New Sexual Tolerance* (Colorado Springs: Multnomah, 2008), 82.

25. I would define acceptance into the fellowship as encouraging involvement in the faith community, which would include attendance at worship services, Bible studies, small groups, and other church-related activities. Full membership, however, would still be dependent on meeting the specific spiritual criteria set forth by the church leadership and/or denomination. As outlined in Scripture, an even higher set of spiritual and behavioral criteria are required for those called into church leadership (1 Timothy 3:1–13; Titus 1:5–9).

Chapter 8

1. This story describes the same situation as Tim's story ("Controlled by Crystal Meth") in chapter 6, but from the perspective of his wife, Rachel.

Chapter 9

1. Richard J. Foster and Gayle D. Beebe, *Longing for God: Seven Paths of Christian Devotion* (Downers Grove, IL: InterVarsity, 2009), 140.

2. John Piper, *The Purifying Power of Living by Faith in Future Grace* (Sisters, OR: Multnomah, 1995), 386.

3. The biblical text often makes reference to the heart and kidneys as the seat of the mind and emotions. In fact, the Hebrew word for kidneys (*kelayot*) is translated as "mind" in the New American Standard Bible. For a review of the ancient understanding of the kidneys' role in

thoughts and behavior, see Garabed Eknoyan, "The kidneys in the Bible: What happened?" *Journal of the American Society of Nephrology* 16 (2005): 3464–71.

4. R. Shane Tubbs et al., "Roots of neuroanatomy, neurology, and neurosurgery as found in the Bible and Talmud," *Neurosurgery* 63 (2008): 156–62.

5. Robert A. J. Gagnon, "Scriptural Perspectives on Homosexuality and Sexual Identity," *Journal of Psychology and Christianity* 24 (2005): 298.